IMAGES
of America

HISTORIC
BEACON

BEACON'S MAIN STREET, C. 1910. Authors' Note: The most difficult challenge associated with writing *Historic Beacon* was narrowing our selection of photographs to those which are contained in its pages. With a few exceptions, the images cover the period from the 1870s to World War II—a timeframe during which our community took its form, prospered, and found its identity.

IMAGES
of America

HISTORIC
BEACON

Robert J. Murphy and Denise Doring VanBuren

ARCADIA

First printed in 1998.
Reprinted in 2003.

Published by Arcadia Publishing,
an imprint of Tempus Publishing, Inc.
2A Cumberland Street
Charleston, SC 29401

Printed in Great Britain.

Library of Congress Catalog Card Number: 98-86902

For all general information contact Arcadia Publishing at:
Telephone 843-853-2070
Fax 843-853-0044
E-Mail sales@arcadiapublishing.com

For customer service and orders:
Toll-Free 1-888-313-2665

Visit us on the internet at http://www.arcadiapublishing.com

In memory of my parents, Elizabeth J. and Robert W. Murphy.
R.J.M.

In celebration of my sons, Schuyler, Troy, and Brett VanBuren.
D.D.VB.

CONTENTS

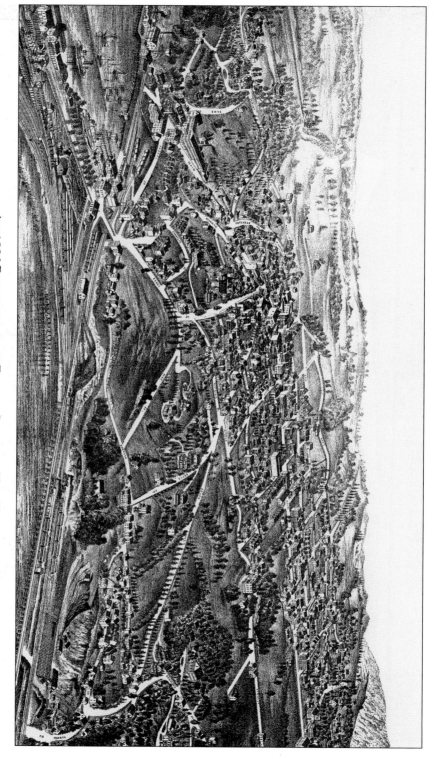

An 1886 Burleigh Map of Fishkill Landing, New York.

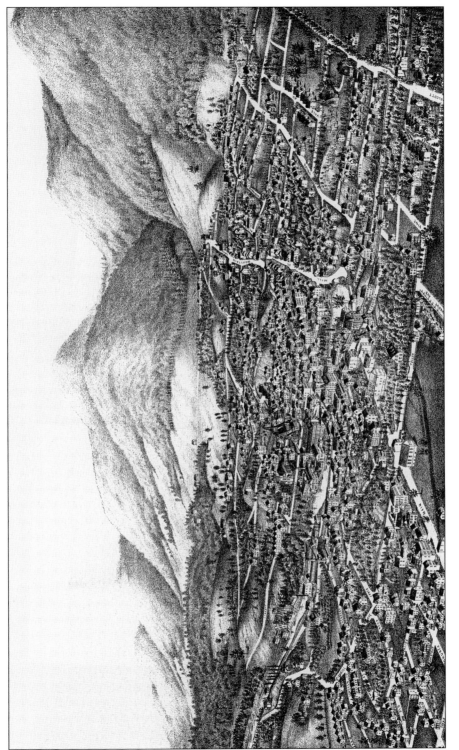

AN 1886 BURLEIGH MAP OF MATTEAWAN, NEW YORK.

INTRODUCTION

This is as fine a river as can be found
and as pleasant a land as one need tread upon.

—Robert Juet, Crew Member
The Half Moon, 1609

On a calm, windless night in 1609, Capt. Henry Hudson and crew floated down the northern river, their quest for a shorter route to the East Indies now but a disappointment. *The Half Moon* dropped anchor at the mouth of the Fishkill Creek, where crew member Robert Juet so described within his journal the land we know today as the city of Beacon. How "pleasant" our land must have seemed, lying undisturbed in the shadow of the highlands and sloping to the wide bay of a great river.

A century after Juet's visit, our first permanent white settlers, Roger and Catheryna Brett, likely experienced the same reaction when they arrived to carve the first homestead, agriculture, and business enterprise from the land. Catheryna had inherited from her father, Francis Rombout, a third of the original Rombout Patent—85,000 acres granted by charter from the Royal Governor and negotiated from the Wappinger Native Americans in 1683.

Widowed with three young sons by 1716, Madam Brett courageously remained in the "wilderness," and unlike patroons to the north, encouraged permanent settlement through the sale of her lands to families from New York and Long Island. Her home, inhabited by seven generations of her descendants, stands within the city limits as the oldest building in Dutchess County—and a testament to Madam Brett's sacrifice and accomplishment.

In time, two separate communities would grow and prosper in the vicinity of the Brett Homestead. On the waterfront, the bustling riverport of Fishkill Landing was strategically located at the crossroads of the era's main artery of transportation (the Hudson River) and the heavily traveled route that brought settlers from New England west to seek the adventure of an expanding nation. By the early 1800s, neighboring Matteawan had emerged as a thriving factory community, its numerous mills powered by the falling rapids of the Fishkill Creek.

Fishkill Landing was formally incorporated as a village in 1864, and Matteawan in 1886. Though each distinct in its own right, the twin villages began to grow together—literally—and shared a contiguous Main Street. Historical records indicate that street meetings were held as early as February 1864 to form one large village, but it was not until 1910 that a formal committee met for the purpose. Contentious issues included a fear of higher taxes and a name for the new city (the original Charter Committee favoring "Melzingah"). Finally on May 15, 1913, legislation was finally signed by Gov. William Sulzer to merge the two Hudson River villages into the City of Beacon—a name drawn from the signal fire built atop Mount Beacon during the American Revolution and chosen in a voter referendum.

We believe another side to the history of our city will emerge from the pages of this book, in stories of the men and women who settled our neighborhoods, built the landmarks of our community, and manned Beacon's factories. Much historical emphasis and a good deal of nostalgia have been placed on the Mount Beacon Incline Railway and the Newburgh-Beacon Ferry, but it's the story of ordinary men and women who make our tale one worth telling. For they and their descendants—recognizing that ours is indeed "as pleasant a land as one need tread upon"—created Beacon, a community with a storied past and a promising future.

One
HIGH ATOP
MOUNT BEACON

For centuries the mountain has stood watch like a sentinel over this patch of valley and its people. Our connections to the mountain our ancestors called Beacon Hill are both historic and symbolic. The history dates back to the Revolution, when beacons were lit there to warn of a potential British invasion. And when the two villages beneath came together, they naturally chose the mountain as a namesake and a symbol for their new city. But it took a manmade enterprise—the Mount Beacon Incline Railway—to bring city and mountain before the world.

POSTCARD VIEW OF MOUNT BEACON INCLINE, C. 1905. In its heyday the Mount Beacon Incline Railway was the most popular day-trip vacation spot in the Hudson Valley, attracting more than 3 million visitors in the 75 years of its operation. The picture postcard craze and the incline both arrived on the American scene at about the same time. The resort proved to be a popular postcard subject as well, with more than one hundred different mountain scenes transposed onto postcards.

CONSTRUCTION OF MOUNT BEACON MONUMENT, 1900. The obeliscal monument of masonry and stone standing on the highest point of the mountain is the Mount Beacon Monument, built to commemorate the burning of signal fires there during the Revolution to warn the valley militia of an upriver invasion by the British. Erected by the Melzingah Chapter of the Daughters of the American Revolution, the monument originally stood 27 feet tall and was built with rock gathered at the site.

PATH TO MOUNT BEACON MONUMENT, C. 1905. Soon after its dedication on July 4, 1900, the Mount Beacon Monument was a favorite hiking destination for local townspeople climbing the mountain. But when the Mount Beacon Incline opened in 1902, the monument became a must-see attraction for tourists strolling along the mountaintop. The hike from the casino to the monument was about a half-mile, rising along a rocky path with added-on wooden staircases to help the unsteady get over the steeper parts.

MOUNT BEACON BACKDROP, C. 1902. Weldon Weston and Henry George of New Hampshire had a vision for Mount Beacon. In the 1890s the two often climbed to its summit and there dreamed of someday building a mountaintop resort where tourists could view the vistas of the beautiful Hudson Valley. In 1900, Weston and George made dream become reality by persuading investors from Maine and New Hampshire to form the Mount Beacon-on-Hudson Association in order to build the Mount Beacon Incline.

INCLINE UNDER CONSTRUCTION, 1902. In October of 1901, 73 men from the Mohawk Construction Company of Mohawk, New York, began the construction of the Mount Beacon Incline Railway. The task was arduous—the pack mules could haul only 24 bricks per load to the top—yet the tracks were in place by late March. The design and the engineering of the railway had been done by the Otis Elevator Company of Yonkers. The total cost of the enterprise was $165,000.

STREETCARS AT MOUNT BEACON, 1902. The railroad, the steamboat, and the ferry were links in a chain of transport that brought the first tourists to the new mountain resort. The final, indispensable link connecting the river to the mountain was the inter-village streetcar. The steamboats docked in Newburgh, passengers then transferred onto the ferry to Fishkill Landing where they boarded trolleys to the incline. "Take the Red Flag Trolley to Mount Beacon" was the final direction the tourist needed.

TROLLEYS OFF-LOADING PASSENGERS AT INCLINE, 1902. The trolley route from the river to the mountain was about a 15-minute ride, rambling over the straightway of Main Street and then onto the zigzag turns on the hill roads of Matteawan. When the incline opened, the streetcar company had to lay 3,500 feet of new track to the mountain. Suddenly, quiet little back streets like Washington, Prospect, and Vail became busy trolley roads carrying thousands of tourists through the neighborhood.

INCLINE'S OPENING DAY, MAY 30, 1902. On a hot, sunny Memorial Day in 1902, a large crowd gathered at the foot of the mountain to be part of the grand opening of the Mount Beacon Incline Railway. More than 1,400 fares were sold that holiday, due in part to the Central Hudson Steamboat ads, placed in New York City papers, which offered an excursion to the mountain and return to the city for $1. All told, 60,000 people rode the incline during that opening season of 1902.

TICKET OFFICE AT INCLINE'S BASE STATION, C. 1905. The round-trip fare up and down the mountain on the cars was 25¢. The excursion rate from Newburgh for the ferry, trolley, and incline was only 45¢. Though your wait in the crowded lines at the base station for your turn to get a seat could be uncomfortable, it was not usually long. The management advertised they could accommodate about 60 passengers at a time, five hundred or more in an hour, if need be.

CARS PASSING ON SWITCH, MOUNT BEACON INCLINE, MATTEAWAN, N

CARS AT THE SWITCH, C. 1905. The incline extended 2,000 feet from the base to the top, rising in places 68 feet in a 100-foot length—hence the claim of its unique steepness. Otis Elevator ingeniously devised a single-track, balanced-car system whereby the car coming down, held by a hoist cable coming from the powerhouse, was perfectly counterbalanced by the car going up. The cars met a turnout, each car switching briefly to its own track, then both returning to the main line.

CAR NEARING SUMMIT, C. 1905. The cars were built by the Ramapo Iron Works of Hilburn, New York, and were 33 feet long, with nine benches to seat 54. Passengers sat facing the river during the four-and-a-half minute climb to the top. To prevent a breakaway, each car had a special braking device which, upon overspeed, released a set of steel jaws to grip the tracks' guardrails and stop the runaway. No major accidents were recorded in 75 years of operation.

CASINO AND POWERHOUSE ON MOUNT BEACON, C. 1902. The summit of the mountain was laid out like a park, with fountains, walks, pavilions, and summer cottages. The center of attraction was the Casino, a restaurant and dance hall with limited sleeping quarters on its top floor. The views from the summit were spectacular. And the mountain air, at 1,539 feet above sea level, was said to be always ten degrees cooler than the valley below and immune from fleas and mosquitoes.

THE CASINO, C. 1902. The Casino was a two-story building with a 12-foot-wide wrap-around piazza. On its roof was the observation deck equipped with coin-operated telescopes. Mounted on the roof's cupola was a 36" reflector searchlight, powerful enough to reach the big steamers sailing the Hudson at night below. Also on the roofline facing the river was a sign with huge letters 10 feet tall by 6 feet wide spelling out "MT. BEACON"—large enough to be seen by river traffic miles away.

BEACONCREST HOTEL AND CASINO, C. 1909. The open season for the incline ran about 150 days—from May to mid-October. Each passing year the resort became more popular, with its ridership averaging about 90,000 fares a year. With this strong base of steady business, in 1908 the resort's management built the Beaconcrest Hotel, a three-story building close by the Casino with 75 guest chambers. Rates were $2.50 per day or $15 per week. With the addition of this hotel, Mount Beacon became a vacation spot of worldwide attraction.

BEAUTIFUL BABY CONTEST ON MOUNT BEACON, 1919. "Mt. Beacon: the most glamorous spot for dining and dancing in the Hudson Valley"—that ad could apply to beauty contests, too. The Beautiful Baby Contest of 1919 was such an example, where the first prize to the prettiest baby was $30 in gold. In 1934, the Casino was the setting for another beauty contest, Miss Mount Beacon. Helen Dolson of Beacon won that title and then went on to become Miss Empire State. She would finish as first runner-up in the Miss Atlantic States Pageant in Boston.

AMUSEMENT PARK ATOP MOUNT BEACON, 1905. Away from the spectacular views of the valley, more pedestrian diversions awaited visitors to the mountaintop. Along the walkways behind the Casino, strollers passed by carnival tents, concession stands, and gaming tables. On these paths a tourist could stop and have his picture taken on tintype, visit a small menagerie, or hire out a donkey and explore the trails back to the reservoir.

COTTAGES ON MOUNT BEACON, C. 1910. By 1910 a thriving cottage colony had developed on Mount Beacon. On the slopes behind the Casino, summer residents leased land from the incline management and built privately owned cottages. These dwellings ranged from primitive to plush, some with whimsical names attached, like Miss Etta Williams's "Up-A-Nuff," and her mother's "Up-Hi-Er." Senator Stuhr of New Jersey built his ornate cottage, "Sans Souci," complete with the first piano on the mountain, brought there, of course, on the incline.

CASINO AND BEACONCREST HOTEL, C. 1908. The 16th of October 1927, had been a warm cloudy day atop Mount Beacon. More than seven hundred people had enjoyed the resort that Sunday, when shortly past midnight, after the last patrons had gone down the incline, fire broke out in the Casino. The siren of the Mase Hook and Ladder firehouse awoke the city to "a spectacle gorgeously awful to behold." A bucket brigade of firemen could save only the powerhouse. The Casino and hotel lay in ruins.

OUTSIDE THE NEW CASINO, C. 1930. The disastrous $400,000 fire of 1927 signaled the end of the Golden Era of Mount Beacon. Ironically, the year before was the resort's best ever, with more than 110,000 people riding the incline. From the ruins, manager John B. Lodge vowed to rebuild, and on May 13, 1928, the new Casino opened. Along with the usual dining and dancing, something new was offered—radio station WOKO began broadcasting "The Voice From the Clouds" from its studio in the Casino high atop Mount Beacon.

CAR WITHOUT A ROOF, C. 1963. The same cable car was twice destroyed by fire in separate incidents on the incline. On August 2, 1936, a brush fire at night burned 250 feet of track, causing passengers to jump for their lives as their descending car passed through the flames, caught fire, and derailed. The car was rebuilt without a roof. On November 10, 1967, fire destroyed the base station and let loose that same car without a roof to travel aflame 300 feet up the tracks. It was rebuilt again without a roof.

DESCENDING MOUNT BEACON, 1946. During the Depression, business on the incline went in a steady downward spiral. Hard times closed Beacon's streetcar system in 1930, its trolleys replaced by buses. New roads and more cars soon displaced travel by boat and rail. With the consequent fewer visitors, the incline staggered through the 1930s, then recovered somewhat in the 1940s, when by then it was the last operating incline in the Northeast. The last good year was 1949, when 50,000 fares were sold.

INCLINE AS SKI-LIFT, 1967. The incline's season usually ran from Memorial Day to Columbus Day. In the 1940s, however, the cable cars saw winter duty, carrying skiers to the top of rough ski trails on Mount Beacon. This use peaked in 1947, when 2,200 skiers rode the incline in one week in February. When the Dutchess Ski Area opened in the mid-1960s with trails adjacent to the incline, the cars again were used for a few seasons to taxi skiers to the top, only to be replaced by a chairlift in 1968.

MOUNT BEACON INCLINE, 1965. After being managed by the Lodge family for 50 years, the Mount Beacon Incline was sold in 1963. Under new management, the incline's fortunes worsened with slumping business and legal squabbles over tax matters. Operating only intermittently in the 1970s, the cable cars made their last run in February 1978, carrying hang gliders to the summit. Fires on the mountain in 1981 and 1983 destroyed the Casino, the powerhouse, the two cars, and the tracks.

Two
OPEN FOR BUSINESS

In 1889, members of the Matteawan and Fishkill-on-Hudson Board of Trade compiled a 35-page book to attract other investors to their community. "It has excellent churches and schools; a circulating library; two newspapers; a hospital; water works; electric light; gas works; a national bank and two savings banks; a good stage line; good stores and mercantile establishments of all kinds; fire department, etc. etc.—what city of 20,000 inhabitants has more?" they asked. And indeed, from the visitor's arrival at the landing all the way through Matteawan, a walk up Main Street did seem to prove that the twin villages had it all.

LANDING AT FISHKILL. Our community's roots run deepest to its origins as a Hudson River landing. During the early 1700s, settlers on the western side of the river trekked from as far as 20 miles inland—and then paddled across in rowboats—to have their grain ground at Madam Brett's mill. The ferry, chartered in 1743, was an impetus to growth at the riverfront, and commerce prospered in its wake.

FLANNERY'S HOTEL, APRIL 9, 1898. After a full year of costly renovation, John Flannery boasted in 1888 that his hotel was "one of the most commodious and comfortable now to be found along the river." The ground floor had a reading room, bar, private dining room, public restaurant, kitchen, barbershop, laundry, and a room where traveling salesman could display their wares. Rooms on the two upper floors featured "hot and cold" water; a large barn and stables adjoined the hotel.

FLANNERY'S HOTEL BAR. A grand character from our past, John Flannery was an Irish immigrant with a lifelong boast that at 19, he owned his own home, his own racehorse, and had $500 in the bank. He started his business in Fishkill Landing at age 25, though his truelove would always remain horse racing. Flannery's horses, seen in photographs above his bar, were famed across the state. His favorite was Mike W., who ran a 1.59-mile in 1905 to win a coveted victory.

BANK SQUARE. As commerce spread up the hill from the riverfront, the hub of Fishkill Landing became "Bank Square," also known as the Five Corners—the intersection of Main Street, North and South Avenues, with Ferry and Beekman Streets. During the prosperous first decade of the 20th century, Bank Square was home to the Fishkill National Bank (located there since 1863), Samuel Beskin's Department Store (the first in the twin villages), and the Fishkill Landing Post Office and Police Station. However, like the clang of the trolleys seen in both of these turn-of-the-century postcards, this once thriving block is now but a memory. Urban Renewal demolitions in the late 1960s and early 1970s leveled the neighborhood, leaving just the intersection of Main Street and Route 9D in its place.

THREE MAIN STREET SHOPS, C. 1900. In the era before one-stop shopping supermarkets, this Main Street row of storefronts surely afforded some efficiency to local customers. Thomas Talbot's fish and oyster house operated at 159 Main Street; next door, George Knapp conducted affairs at his meat market; and, finally, at 163 Main, shoppers could peruse dry goods and groceries at the establishment of Charles E. Martin. Knapp doubled duty as coroner in Fishkill Landing, and Martin served as secretary at the nearby Mechanic's Savings Bank.

THREE MAIN STREET SHOPS, C. 1930. Central Hudson would eventually occupy the 163 Main storefront. The first electricity in the villages was supplied in 1893 by the Carroll's Electric Company, formed by proprietors of the Carroll Hat Works. That firm combined with the Citizens Street Railway Company in 1901. In 1922, they were folded into the Southern Dutchess Gas & Electric Company, whose predecessor companies had operated manufactured gas works within the villages since 1858. They became part of Central Hudson in 1926.

MAIN AT CROSS, 1928. A building boom like no other hit Beacon in 1928 and 1929. "Never before," the *Beacon News* reported, "have so many structures been underway." Being built or rebuilt were: the East Main Street bridge, the Mount Beacon Casino, the South Avenue School, the National Biscuit Company plant, and two new banks on Main Street—the Matteawan Savings and the Mechanic Savings (the latter's scaffolding evident mid-block). The two banks would merge in 1935 to become Beacon Savings Bank, which eventually folded into Albany Savings Bank.

McCallin's Meat Market, c. 1890. By 1892, Frank McCallin's business required five men and the constant use of four wagons to deliver daily orders to customers. McCallin had purchased the Excelsior Market in 1883 from W.J. Ollivet, who had started the business in 1876. Beef, mutton, veal, lamb, poultry, and game "in their season" were available, as well as corned beef, pork, and smoked meats—and all were on open display for the customer's inspection. McCallin advertised to spare "no pains to satisfy the purchasing public."

A.C. Smith and Company, c. 1903. As a young man in Newburgh, Chester Bond became a plumber's apprentice under A.C. Smith. So successful was that apprenticeship that he was given the opportunity to run and ultimately buy Smith's Fishkill Landing operation. Bond, who remained active in the business until his death at 89, also became a leading citizen: trustee of a local bank, chief of Tompkin's Hose, and father to a future mayor. Yet, out of affection and respect for Smith, he never changed the concern's name.

W.H. Rogers & Company, c. 1898. All manner of stoves, ranges, tinware, hardware, cutlery, woodenware, farm implements, and even "house furnishings" could be found at the 168 Main Street premises of W.H. Rogers. The business, founded in 1858, sold its goods ("all of the best quality") within a radius of 60 miles. According to the September 3, 1898, issue of *The Fishkill Standard*, the establishment's success was due to "the superiority of goods handled and the honorable and straightforward methods which have characterized its dealings."

ROBERT VAN TINE, C. 1910. For generations of local residents, Van Tine's was the single source for local and out-of-town newspapers and magazines. Robert T. Van Tine, son of John Van Tine (superintendent of the Fishkill Landing Corliss Engine Company), began the business near the intersection of Cross Street in 1880 as a men's "furnishings" store. Shortly after, he moved it to 177 Main Street and began to trade exclusively in stationery. His son Harry photographed the local scenes from which many of our early postcards were made.

MCFARLANE'S DRUG STORE, C. 1928. Twenty-cent chocolate sundaes were on order at the soda fountain of McFarlane's Drug Store, later Nerrie's, at 163 Main Street in Fishkill Landing. L.J. Scofield, L.W. Scofield, and J. Scott Nerrie stand ready to serve in a scene that was invariably played out in small drugstores like this one on main streets across America during the era.

HOLLAND HOTEL. The Christmas season of 1894 was made especially bright with the opening of the Hotel Holland, and many local residents celebrated with a special dinner in the main dining room of the new establishment. A handsome, three-story building of red brick with blue stone trimmings, the hotel was owned by William Gordon. There were ten fireplaces (each with oak mantel and tile hearth) in the principal rooms, a billiard room, and dining room, while guest rooms were furnished in North Carolina pine.

BEACON DAIRY, C. 1930. In the darkness of early morning, milkmen Lou Dinan and William Morse could be found driving their wagons through the streets of Beacon, delivering milk—often to families unable to pay during the Great Depression. Tough times, in fact, closed the business. Then, in 1936, Hopewell Junction dairyman J.C. Penney arrived on the scene. Following installation of a $25,000 milk pasteurizing system, his Emmadine Farm was soon turning out 6,000 quarts of milk a day for customers from Peekskill to Poughkeepsie.

ACADEMY OF MUSIC, 1905. Forerunner to the modern movie theater, Peatties' Academy of Music was one of two variety houses in the twin villages of the last century. Built in 1894 on Main Street between South Walnut and South Elm, the Academy once welcomed such notables as John Philip Sousa, the March King. In later years, vaudeville acts played there and then silent movies when it was known as the State Theater. The building was destroyed by fire in 1926.

FAULKNER'S SALOON, 1877. The Temperance Movement had few conversions here, as the 1879 local paper hinted: "It is almost a useless effort—someone counted 160 saloons from the end of Long Wharf to the mountains." Among them was John Faulkner's, offering a "2 for 1" special at its Main Street location (site of today's Grand Union supermarket). Yet the liquor traffic did ease the local tax burden; in 1893, the town granted 95 licenses and collected $4,140 in tax revenues.

SCHOONMAKER'S STORE SITE. When Schoonmaker's store on the corner of Main and North Chestnut Streets was being built, no mention was made that boxing legend John L. Sullivan once had his training camp on that very spot. What mattered was Beacon now had a real department store—one to rival those of Newburgh and Poughkeepsie—to shop in that Christmas season of 1929. Schoonmaker's offered upscale shopping, lunches at its soda fountain, and Toyland, where you found the only Santa in-person in town.

MAIN STREET AT ELIZA STREET. The twin villages literally grew together, though their center area long remained undeveloped, owing to its tendency to flood—a fact which also gave rise to the nickname given to generations of its residents: "Swamp Angels." Though the villages were merging, their citizens would remain, in some respects, distinct. For years to come, those who grew up near the waterfront were branded "River Rats," while inhabitants in the east end boasted of being "Mountaineers."

BURNET'S CIGAR STORE, C. 1880. Like most young boys a century ago, these youngsters probably had little choice but to work, and were likely apprenticed in the trade. In an 1890 edition of the *Fishkill Standard*, one local resident recounted details of his 1844 five-year indenture to "faithfully serve said master, his secrets keep, his lawful commands everywhere readily obey." In return, he was taught the profession and provided "sufficient meat, drink, washing, mending, lodging" and paid $20 per year.

DIBBLE HOUSE. Warren S. Dibble purchased a Matteawan hotel in 1877 and improved it to 75 rooms and a commodious stable. Seven years later, with roller skating the latest craze, he built the Matteawan Skating Rink across Main Street. But interest in the sport declined rapidly and the building was converted into the Dibble Opera House by 1886. There, in a 1,300-seat hall, he furnished "a high-class of entertainment to an appreciative public." The Beacon Theater was later constructed on the site.

C.H. HOYSRADT, UNDERTAKER. Like many other tradesmen once associated with woodworking, C.H. Hoysradt was proof that just about anyone with a woodshed was liable to put out an "Undertaker" sign. Mr. Hoysradt, whose shop was located at 467 Main Street in Matteawan, could not only sell you a couch or a casket but he also doubled as a justice of the peace. "Judge" Hoysradt, fourth from the left, resided upstairs and accepted calls "night or day."

BROWN BLOCK, C. 1889. William Brown operated men's stores at 466 and 470 Main Street and served as president of the villages' Board of Trade in the 1890s. In the latter part of that decade, the YMCA operated on the second floor of the block. Its "commodious rooms" included a parlor, library, gameroom, and gymnasium, "which supply social, physical, intellectual, and spiritual aid and comfort to an interested class of patrons numbering from 200 to 400 per week."

33

MAIN AT TIORONDA, C. 1920S. In the days before superhighways and shopping malls, every community's main street was its central attraction—as evident in the number of prosperous shops in business at the bend in Beacon's east end. A 1930 city directory lists 23 apparel, 89 food, seven drug, and five jewelry stores in business, as well as seven florists and 19 restaurants. A 1930 retail trade census lists 222 establishments open for business, including 12 lumber- and building yards.

CIRCUS WAGONS, 1910. While the arrival of a circus was big news in any small town, it had particular significance here. Isaac Van Amburgh, who was born here in 1808, was the first wild-animal trainer. Following a circus tour through Europe, which included a command performance before Queen Victoria, Van Amburgh introduced the ornate, European-style circus wagon to America. Van Amburgh's legacy is somewhat ironic, for had his eyesight been better, he may have succeeded in the tailor's trade that he was once apprenticed in Fishkill Landing!

Three

ON THE FACTORY FLOOR

"Without Matteawan, Americans would almost go hatless, and a really fine American carpet would be unknown. People from other manufacturing towns say that they do not know or appreciate what dull times are in Matteawan. May they long remain in blissful ignorance," wrote a reporter for the *Daily Graphic of New York* in 1879. Over the course of a century, scores of products were produced and thousands employed within the factories of Beacon. And though "blissful ignorance" regrettably did fade with the exodus of her largest employers, the lasting legacy of Beacon's glory days as a manufacturing boomtown will remain forever.

MATTEAWAN COMPANY, 1832. Founded as a cotton mill in 1814 by Philip A. Hone and Peter A. Schenck, the Matteawan Company was our first factory. Reminiscing in 1874, two local residents who had worked there as boys recalled that "(i)n those days, the girls could stop their looms and go down to the fountain and wash their hands and faces without getting a scolding." The building was expanded over time, and used to manufacture cotton, wool, sugar, refining machinery, baby carriages, electric blankets, and hats.

SCHENCK GRISTMILL, LATE 1880S. Generations of local farmers brought their grain to the creek side near Churchill Street to be ground at a gristmill started in the mid-1700s and operational until fire struck in 1915. The Schenck mill is long gone, its foundation today the site of a wrecking yard for junked cars. But for more than 150 years, "the highest cash price paid" could be found here for farmers, while customers in turn purchased "superfine family flour" and other products.

NEW YORK RUBBER COMPANY. Charles Wolcott began New York Rubber Company in 1858 in a cotton mill built on the creek in 1841-42. By the 1870s, it boasted of being the only factory in the country producing rubber toys, and creator of the longest rubber belt ever made: 268 feet long, weighing 2,214 pounds (for a St. Louis grain elevator). Perhaps the factory's oddest specialty was the manufacture of rubber hands and feet—in great demand following the Civil War.

ROTHERY FILE WORKS, C. 1880s. John Rothery is considered the father of American file manufacturing. Born in Sheffield, England, he arrived in Matteawan in 1835, and set about making cast steel files to rival those made in his homeland. And indeed, the factory produced what came to be regarded as the first and finest files in America. The building burned on October 28, 1886, and there is speculation that the fire led to the formal formation of the villages' fire companies.

ROTHERY FILE WORKERS, C. 1870. The Rotherys rebuilt the file works, and workmen (and boys) like these carried on its reputation for quality through two more generations and six decades. But the family "had no faith in machine-made files, and refused to thus equip their plant. They were eventually compelled to give up the business, as they could not compete in price with the machine-made file," noted one local historian. The building, which survived through several subsequent uses, was later a silk mill.

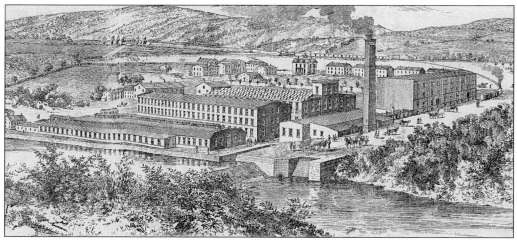

GROVEVILLE MILLS, 1879. The Groveville property was acquired in 1876 by merchant A.T. Stewart, considered the wealthiest man in America at the time. Stewart began creation of a "community" with the construction of carpet mills and houses for workers. In so doing, he cut down the grove of oaks which gave the property its name. By the early 1880s, more than seven hundred hands were employed here; but a decade later, the firm moved to Yonkers. A Swiss lace company and the Lewittes Furniture Company were among the later tenants.

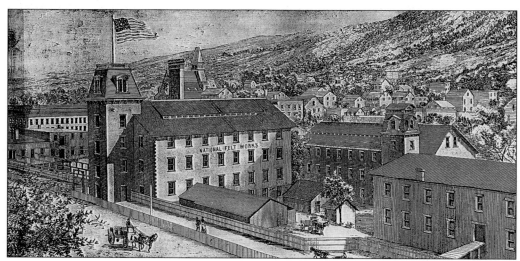

NATIONAL FELT WORKS, 1879. Like many other factory buildings that weathered boom-and-bust economic cycles, this creek side property evolved through a number of varied uses. Located amongst the holdings of the original Matteawan Company, it was once home to the Seamless Clothing Manufacturing Company, which employed 95 men in 1860. John Falconer & Co. later made felt goods here, as did Falconer, Carroll & Company, who operated the business before the century's turn under the name of the National Felt Works.

FISHKILL LANDING MACHINE COMPANY ADVERTISEMENT, 1879. Though best known for its Corliss Engine, the Fishkill Landing Machine Company manufactured steam engines of all kinds beginning in 1853, and even made cannons during the Civil War. The factory was located near the river—ideally adjacent to the Hudson River Railroad, enabling it to ship its engines all over the world. It was ironic, then, that it was the New York Central line that bought out the business in 1912 in order to accommodate its new four-track system. More than one hundred workers lost their jobs.

FISHKILL LANDING MACHINE COMPANY.

(ESTABLISHED 1853.)

Fishkill-on-the-Hudson, N.Y.

Manufacturers of

STEAM ENGINES,

BOILERS,

And Machinery

OF EVERY DESCRIPTION.

THE MILLS AGRICULTURAL ENGINE.　　THE CELEBRATED

LOOMIS AUTOMATIC CUT-OFF ENGINE,

AND THE

MILLS PORTABLE ENGINE.

MILO SAGE, President.　　　JAS. L. TELLER, Secretary.

ROBERT I. HALGIN, Superintendent.

NATIONAL FELT WORKS, C. 1880. A factory chimney towered above the work yard of the felt works, where five hundred men were employed for the manufacture of "felt hats, seamless skirts, and druggets" (the last a woven wool fabric used for clothing), according to the 1880 village directory. The white items scattered about the enclosed area are assumed to be hat molds. The Fountain Square store sign in the distance reads "William B. Myer, Groceries & Provisions, Crockery & Glass, Dealer in Willoware."

ONE EAST MAIN STREET, 1923. Called Carrolls, Eli Berman, or Bobrich, this factory has been home to makers of (among others) straw hats, furniture, baby carriages, and electric blankets. But its heritage is a blend of old and new: the coupling of the oldest building on the creek with the youngest. The south side of the building contains the old stone mill built by Schenck and Hone in 1814; the 1912 brick building was erected by the Schrader Hat Company to create the nation's most modern straw hat manufactory.

FACTORY COMPLEX AT EAST MAIN STREET, C. 1930. These buildings were originally an annex of the old Matteawan Company located across the street. In 1864, the Matteawan Manufacturing Company, our first hat factory, occupied the main building and employed nearly five hundred hatters. Later, Willard H. Mase ran the concern when it was known as the Mase Hat Shop. The roundhouse in the foreground was once the home of Horatio N. Swift's Machine Shop, manufacturing site of America's first lawnmowers. Braendly's Dye Works later occupied the site.

40

TIORONDA HAT SHOP WORKERS, C. 1880. Youngsters toiled side by side with experienced hatters during Beacon's heyday as the "Hat Capital of New York State." Only Danbury, Connecticut, produced more hats in post-Civil War America. Lewis Tompkins is generally credited with having spurred the hat-making industry here, establishing his lower Main Street Dutchess Hat Shop in 1874. A lack of proper water facilities to cleanse and dye wool at that location prompted him to build the Tioronda Works along the Fishkill Creek in 1879.

DUTCHESS HAT WORKS, C. 1880. Having studied the successful factory methods of Europe, Lewis Tompkins became one of America's largest and most successful hat manufacturers. Within two decades, his booming factories employed a combined 650 workers. His Dutchess Hat Works alone was turning out 450 dozen felt hats per day in the early 1890s. Three factory floors (each measuring 175 feet x 300 feet) were dedicated to the enterprise, and its products were sold across the nation from a Broadway showroom in New York City.

FINISHING ROOM AT A TOMPKINS'S HAT FACTORY, C. 1880. Also owner of the Hudson Straw Works, Tompkins was one of the villages' most respected citizens. And despite what were obviously harsh working conditions, his employees never unionized. His obituary read, "His fair dealing has been the means of his getting the best service from his employees and keeping their regard and esteem. None outside of his family mourn his death with keener regret than those who have worked for him in any capacity."

GENUINE PANAMA HAT COMPANY, C. 1930S. The height of Beacon's hatting industry occurred between 1920 and 1940, when 11 major factories turned out hundreds of thousands of hats in scores of styles—including the straw variety produced at this Verplank Avenue factory. The hat's decline in fashion, the Great Depression, a six-year strike in the 1930s, and cheaper foreign imports all contributed to the industry's decline; factories which once produced hats sold worldwide, closed for business one by one.

SCHENCK MACHINERY WORKS, 1882. After 20 years in business in Massachusetts, Samuel B. Schenck arrived in Matteawan in 1851 in order to expand his manufacture of woodworking machinery. He first set up shop in the blacksmith foundry of the Matteawan Company to produce his Woodworth planers. Prosperity induced the shop to larger quarters at the corner of Herbert Street, where 30 workers toiled. The business disappeared from City Directories in the 1890s, though Woodworth planers were still in documented use a century later.

GREEN FUEL ECONOMIZER. Established on 12 acres of land in 1891, the Green Fuel Economizer Company produced an apparatus for "utilizing wasted gases passing from steam boilers to reheat water, thus affording a great savings in coal." At the extensive complex, where four hundred hands were employed, fans, blowers, and heating systems were also produced and then sold worldwide—with particular success in England. It was later Green Fan, and it is now the site of the world-famous Tallix Art Foundry.

JACKSON CARRIAGE WORKS, C. 1870. Begun by William H. Jackson in 1860, the Main Street Jackson Carriage works produced fine carriages, sleighs, and wagons—even sturdy work carts—for more than 60 years. Jackson built his home on the corner of Main and Fishkill Avenue and his factory next door. His first customer was said to have been Mr. Delano of Newburgh—grandfather of President Roosevelt—and his daughter, Mrs. Delano Hitch, to be the last before Jackson retired.

JACKSON CARRIAGE WORKERS, 1872. Posed beneath the center arch of the establishment (still standing near Fishkill Avenue), carriage workers like these cut, planed, and designed the carriages by hand. Every carriage had nine coats of paint and varnish—each rubbed down before the next was applied, and a painted carriage cured for three weeks. From blacksmiths and wood carvers to upholsterers, harness makers and painters, these workers were skilled hand craftsmen.

DUTCHESS TOOL WORKERS, APRIL 23, 1910. Once internationally recognized for its baker's ovens, Dutchess Tool Company was for more than 70 years one of our steadiest employers. The factory was founded by Frank Van Houten in 1886 and by 1891 was located on South Avenue in the old Academy Street School. Besides making bakery machinery (some of which is still in use around the world), Dutchess Tool also made steering apparatus for warships during World War II, for which it earned the Maritime "M" Award for high production standards.

HAMMOND'S SLUG SHOT AND PAINT WORKS, C. 1880. Benjamin Hammond had relocated his insecticide manufacturing business in 1880 from Mount Kisco to Long Dock to find a good shipping port for his wares. By 1900 business was booming; Hammond's 24-page booklet was mailed coast-to-coast and his products shipped as far as New Zealand. His best seller was "Slug Shot," an insecticide for "worms of all sorts." He also sold "Kerosene Emulsion" for caterpillars and "Cattle Comfort" to ward flies off livestock.

DUTCHESS HAT BASEBALL TEAM, 1923. Baseball has been played in Beacon ever since the Civil War. But in the 1920s, when a factory league formed, baseball's local popularity hit its peak. Rivalries between the hat shops and New York Rubber Company, for example, were so intense that, if you could play ball, Dutchess Hat Shop hired you to work at a good salary in their wool shop. Winning the factory league made you champions of the city.

GIRLS BASKETBALL, 1919. The office girls of Green Fuel Economizer were hailed as Hudson Valley Champions, after compiling a 15-1 record in the 1918-1919 season. Local newspapers recounted, "The G.F.E. girls are one of the cleanest and cleverest playing teams in this section of the State and are familiar with all the fine points of the game." Listed from left to right are as follows: (front row) Margaret Pulford and Anna Mitchell; (back row) Anna Bell Lee, Lauretta Kearney, Catherine Lee, and Catherine Morris.

Four

ABOARD THE NEWBURGH-BEACON FERRY

The story of the Newburgh-Beacon Ferry can be told loaded with historical superlatives. It was one of the longest-running ferry lines in America's history, in operation for 220 years, starting back in 1743 when King George granted the original charter. It was arguably the most important ferry of the American Revolution, serving as a vital cross-river transport for men and supplies of Washington's army. And over the years its fleet was composed of some of the best-known ferries to ply the Hudson—ferries such as the *Moses Rodgers*, the *Union*, the *Dutchess*, and the *Orange*. But the lasting story of the ferries remains in the recounted memories of what it was once like to ride on the Newburgh-Beacon Ferry.

LONG DOCK AND THE NEWBURGH-FISHKILL FERRY, C. 1890. For more than two centuries the ferry was a private enterprise, owned by some of the biggest names in Hudson River shipping: men like John Peter DeWindt of Fishkill Landing, who built Long Dock and made our river-front into a navigable port. And Thomas Powell of Newburgh, and especially his son-in-law, Homer Ramsdell, who made the ferry into a successful family business until it was sold in 1956 to the New York State Bridge Authority.

NEW FERRYHOUSE AT FISHKILL LANDING, C. 1892. The busiest and central point of travel in the village of Fishkill Landing was right in front of the Newburgh-Fishkill ferryhouse. There, passengers for the ferry, the New York Central Railroad, and the electric streetcar all commingled. The ferryhouse, distinguished by its picturesque tower and covered walkway leading to the railroad station, was built in 1892 to handle the greater passenger traffic brought on that year by the start of the trolley-car line.

NEW BEACON FERRY TERMINAL, C. 1914. For the Newburgh-Beacon Ferry Company, 1914 would be the last year of large capital investment in the ferry service. In May of 1914 the new Beacon Ferryhouse opened, built on filled-in ground farther out in the river than the old terminal, and of a larger size to accommodate more passengers and modern vehicles. In August of 1914 the company launched the ferryboat *Orange*, the last of the new ferries on the line. With the ferries' demise, the Beacon terminal was razed in 1968.

FERRYBOAT *UNION*, 1875. The Newburgh and Fishkill Ferry Company purchased secondhand in 1860 the ferryboat *Union*, which had been running a route between New York and Brooklyn. The *Union* had a heavy 14-inch-thick hull of oak planks sheathed in copper, giving her the reputation as the best ice-breaking boat between Albany and New York. On October 1, 1878, the *Union* caught fire and sunk in the river at the foot of Washington Street in Newburgh. Divers salvaged her engine, which was put in her replacement, the ferry *City of Newburgh*.

FERRYBOAT *City of Newburgh*, c. 1890s. Built in Newburgh in 1879, the ferry *City of Newburgh* holds the distinction of the boat with the longest years in service in the history of the Newburgh-Beacon Ferry—from 1879 to 1939. The engines of the *City of Newburgh* date back even earlier, having been salvaged from the sunken ferry *Union*. The ferry's last years of service were as a reserve boat, until the *Beacon* arrived to take on that role in 1938. The *City of Newburgh* was withdrawn from service in 1939 and sold for scrap.

FERRYBOAT *Fishkill on Hudson,* **c. 1890s.** Built in Newburgh in 1884, the *Fishkill on Hudson,* like her companion boat *City of Newburgh,* had an iron hull to break through ice barriers. With both of these side-wheeler ferries in operation, the last recorded suspension of winter service due to ice was 1881. In 1915 the *Fishkill on Hudson* was sold to run across the Long Island Sound from New Rochelle to Glen Cove. She was resold again and renamed the *Jamestown* to run between Newport and Jamestown, Rhode Island, in the 1930s.

FERRY AFTER COLLISION, 1884. The ferry *Fishkill on Hudson* began service on the river on May 25, 1884. A month later she was temporarily out of commission after colliding with the day-liner *Vibbard* at her slip in Newburgh. Damage to the boat was minor, but ferry service was interrupted. For the next 80 years, delays from ice jams, mud banks, fog, and breakdowns were part and parcel of the adventure and exasperation of travel by ferry.

FERRY WILLIAM T. HART, C. 1880S. The *William T. Hart* was a huge train transport ferry put into service from 1882 to 1904 to carry cars of the New York and New England Railroad from Fishkill Landing across the Hudson River, there to hook up with the Erie Railroad in Newburgh. The *William T. Hart* was at the time the second-largest ferry in the world—295 feet long. With decks 80 feet wide, the vessel could carry 27 freight cars or 18 passenger cars in each crossing.

FERRYBOAT DUTCHESS, 1914. The first screw-propelled ferryboat in service on the Hudson River above New York was the *Dutchess*, built for the Newburgh-Fishkill Ferry by the local shipyard of Thomas Marvel and Company of Newburgh. With a hull made of steel and a net weight of 405 tons, the 135-foot long *Dutchess* was well suited for winter duty as an icebreaker. Last of the white-painted ferries, the *Dutchess* made her maiden voyage from Newburgh to Fishkill Landing on August 20, 1910.

INTERIOR OF FERRYBOAT *DUTCHESS*, C. 1915. A curious early feature on the ferryboats was separate entryways and seating quarters for men and women. And as the ferries never made U-turns, the men's side of the boat always faced down river, the women's upriver. The separation of the sexes ostensibly was designed so men would have their own smoking section. Ironically, after a fire destroyed the superstructure of the *Dutchess* in July 1961, smoking was banned on all ferries thereafter.

FERRYBOAT *ORANGE*, C. 1960. The ferryboat *Orange* was the sister ship of the *Dutchess*, built in 1914 to her same specifications by the same shipyard, T.S. Marvel and Company of Newburgh. The *Orange* was the first of the red ferries of the fleet—prior to 1914 all of the ferries had been painted white. But the owners decided that for the *Orange*, a "Tuscan red" with an overcoat of varnish would last for two years, whereas the white ferries were dirty from coal soot in just two weeks.

FERRYBOAT *BEACON*, C. 1960. The harsh winters of the 1930s caused frequent delays in ferry service, with either the *Dutchess* or the *Orange* disabled in turn from fighting the ice. In need of a third winter-worthy boat, the Newburgh-Beacon Ferry Company purchased in May 1938 the *Lieutenant Flaherty*, a 174-foot-long, all-steel-built ferry in 1921 for service in Boston Harbor. With a capacity to carry between 40 and 45 cars, the *Lieutenant Flaherty* was to be one of the largest ferries on the Hudson. Now renamed the *Beacon*, she joined the *Orange* and *Dutchess* in regular service in June of 1938.

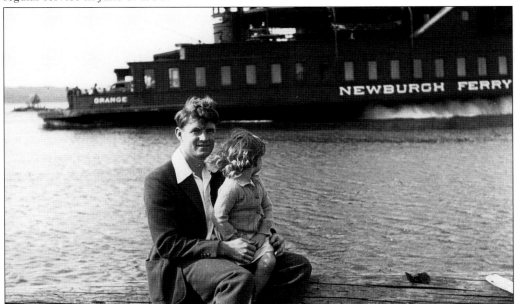

SUMMER'S DAY ON THE FERRY, 1940. In the summertime the ferries often became picnic boats as sightseers and families on a day's outing joined daily commuters to ride back and forth across the river. Both the *Dutchess* and the *Orange* had open upper decks with bench seating, where, for the 10 or 15¢ passenger fare, you could bring your lunch and enjoy the river breezes on a hot summer's day. For some, including Robert W. Murphy and daughter Barbara, it was treat enough to simply enjoy the scene from shore.

THE FERRY AND THE NEW BRIDGE, 1963. After 220 years of continuous service, the era of the Newburgh-Beacon Ferry came to an end with the opening of the Newburgh-Beacon Bridge on November 2, 1963. In the late afternoon of the next day, the *Dutchess* and the *Orange* set out from opposite shores for one last symbolic run. With their whistles blowing in final salute, the sister ferries, with a century of service between them, met at mid-river and then finished their run.

FERRYBOAT DUTCHESS, C. 1945. When the new $22 million Newburgh-Beacon Bridge opened, the Bridge Authority quickly disposed of the ferries. That fall, the *Beacon* and the *Dutchess* were towed down river and sold to a Staten Island salvage yard for $4,700. The *Orange* fared better. Bought by a ferry enthusiast bent on restoring her, the *Orange* went on to make several excursion runs, including one to the New York World's Fair in 1964. But after being vandalized in her Jersey City dock, the *Orange*, too, was scrapped in 1966.

Five
THE TRANSITION OF TRANSPORTATION

The great changes in transportation sweeping across America after the Civil War were to affect the local landscape as well. At the crossover of the new century our villages' streets were crowded with wagon teams, trolley cars, and steam locomotives, all bumping up against each other as we entered the modern age. The image of the horse-and-buggy juxtaposed with the electric streetcar symbolizes the clash of the old with the new. Soon, in the next historical moment, the automobile will appear to squeeze both off the streets forever.

Main Street, Fronting The Railroad. Matteawan, N. Y.

AROUND THE BEND OF MAIN STREET IN MATTEAWAN, C. 1910. The hub of business activity and transportation for the village of Matteawan was located at the bend of Main Street. On or near that curve were the retail shops, post office, library, and two large hat factories. A block down the road was the crossing switch for the trolley lines to Fishkill and Mount Beacon. And the New England Railroad's freight and passenger station was on the bend, so it was commonplace to see a wagon, streetcar, and train pass close by each other.

JAKAB'S BLACKSMITH SHOP, NORTH AVENUE, C. 1915. The 1896 directory for Fishkill Landing and Matteawan lists 22 men with the occupation of blacksmith. Among them was Paul Jakab, who had his smithy on North Avenue near the village limits. In the directory for 1928, now at the end of the horse-and-buggy era, only four blacksmiths are listed. Paul Jakab again was one—in business still by his adapting the carriage repair trade to that of automobile parts replacement.

THE WESTON TRANSFER COMPANY. In 1888, brothers Weldon F. and W.H. Weston (residents of Fishkill Landing and Newburgh, respectively) purchased the Matteawan & Fishkill Landing Stage Line and were soon engaged in a brisk transport business on both sides of the river. While both figured prominently in local transportation concerns, it was Weldon who would originate the idea to build an incline to the top of Mount Beacon, and convince other business partners from their native New Hampshire to help finance the concept.

LOCOMOTIVE ON TRESTLE OVER FISHKILL CREEK ABOVE SUCKER FALLS, 1872. The Dutchess and Columbia's line from Hopewell to Dutchess Junction was operational by late 1869. Just below the New York Rubber Company's factory, the track crossed over the Fishkill Creek on a railroad bridge built near General Howland's Tioronda School. A short distance from there was the terminal at the junction, where for several years in the 1870s the ferryboat *Fanny Garner* transported the railroad's freight across the river to tie in with the Erie line at Newburgh.

RAILROAD TERMINAL AT FISHKILL LANDING, C. 1880S. By 1881 plans were made to replace the Dutchess Junction terminal with an expansive ferry dock and railroad yard in Fishkill Landing. There, the New England Railroad laid tracks parallel to the Hudson River Line and built a dock on filled-in land 200 feet below Long Wharf. By early 1882 the transport ferry *William T. Hart* was carrying freight cars from this new terminal across the river to the Erie Railroad in Newburgh. The dock and terminal lost all importance after a connecting line was built to the Poughkeepsie Railroad Bridge in 1892.

TRAIN AT MATTEAWAN DEPOT, C. 1880. In the spring of 1868, when the Dutchess and Columbia Railroad was laying track for its new line to Dutchess Junction, the proposed roadbed went straight through the middle of the Methodist and Episcopal Church of Matteawan. To make room for the railroad, the church had to be razed and a new one built just down the road and opposite the Howland Library. Where the church had stood, the Matteawan Depot was constructed in 1873, to serve as a passenger and freight station.

TRAIN APPROACHES NEW ENGLAND RAILROAD STATION AFTER SNOWSTORM, 1918. Snowstorms of the past had little affect on the railroads, with the exception of the Blizzard of '88. In his diary, businessman Ben Hammond noted the silence after the big storm: "Not a train whistle to be heard, all trains are stopped. A small train on the New England tracks with two livestock cars of pigs was stalled for two days." The eerie quiet was broken "with the squeaks and moans of those poor animals exposed to the weather."

MATTEAWAN RAILROAD DEPOT, C. 1930. The Matteawan Depot was originally a two-story frame building built in 1873 at a cost of about $3,000—only $1,200 of which was borne by the railroad, the balance paid for by the Village of Matteawan. The depot's lower floor was at track level where freight shipments arrived; the upper floor at street level had a ticket office and waiting room for passengers. A third floor was added after fire destroyed the Dutchess Junction station in 1876 and the railroad had to relocate its offices to Matteawan.

MATTEAWAN RAILROAD DEPOT, C. 1930s. The railroad through Matteawan has had over the years a jumble of owners and line changes. At various times it has been the Dutchess and Columbia; the Newburgh, Dutchess, and Connecticut; the New York and New England; and the New York, New Haven, and Hartford, among others. By the late 1920s the automobile had made passenger train service on this line unprofitable. In 1933 the last rail passengers rode by the Matteawan Depot on the New Haven railbus *Leaping Lena.*

RAILROAD GATEHOUSE AT EAST MAIN STREET CROSSING, C. 1900. The New England Railroad crossed several busy streets as it traversed the village of Matteawan. At two of these intersections the Railroad placed one-man gatehouses and crossing gates: East Main Street and Mill Street (Churchill Street today). The busier was the East Main crossing, for there trolley and rail lines crossed at a right angle. The gatekeeper, usually a disabled railway worker, upon receiving the signal of an approaching train, would lower the gate by hand. This gatehouse was still being manned into the 1940s.

LOOKING NORTH TO BEACON STATION, 1916. By winter of 1916, the New York Central's four-track line at Beacon was in operation. The new system placed the express tracks in the center, with the north- and southbound local tracks to either side. Passenger platforms, accessed by way of a subway from the depot, straddled both local tracks. Two tracks of the Central New England road were nearer the station. The Beacon station and rail yard were at the apex of activity.

NEW YORK CENTRAL DEPOT AT BEACON, 1916. The opening of the New York Central's new passenger depot in November of 1915 was the culmination of three years' work by the railroad to renovate its Beacon station. The two-story brick building contained a ticket office, waiting room, and baggage storeroom, and was a handsome example of early 20th-century railway architecture. After 60 years of use, the station was razed by the Metropolitan Transportation Authority in 1976.

NEW YORK CENTRAL FREIGHT YARD, 1928. The expansion at the Beacon station of the New York Central Railroad began prior to World War I and continued into the early 1920s. With the completion of its four-track line, the Central constructed a freight side-yard east of the train station, near the old Tompkins' Straw Hat Factory at the end of Main Street. In the coming years the yard would be removed as the railroad lost freight business and sought to economize.

TROLLEY CROSSING TEMPORARY RAILROAD BRIDGE, 1915. The transportation hub of the new city of Beacon was just off its waterfront. There, passenger traffic for the ferry, the railroad, and the trolley all converged. By 1915, this area was under renovation: the new ferry terminal had opened recently, the New York Central Railroad was building a new train station, and a new railroad bridge was being constructed. For travelers of the time, first impressions of Beacon were bound to be favorable.

EARLY TROLLEY ON MAIN STREET, NEAR CHESTNUT, C. 1900. The Citizens Street Railway Company in August of 1891 was granted a franchise by the State to run an electric railway from the river in Fishkill Landing to the Union School on Spring Street in Matteawan. The railway opened on August 27, 1892, and proved successful, carrying two thousand to nine thousand passengers a day. Beacon's line was the first electric railway in the Hudson River Valley between New York and Albany, and its success spawned other railways in nearby cities.

CAR BARN, MAIN AND SOUTH CHESTNUT STREETS, C. 1895. The Citizens Street Railway Company had five new cars in service for its opening week and employed eight motormen and 14 conductors to operate the streetcars. Many of these men had been drivers on the old stage line that the trolley was replacing. The cars were run every 7.5 minutes along the route and the fare to any destination was 5¢. More than 720,000 fares were sold on the trolleys that first year.

TROLLEY TO FISHKILL, C. 1900. "Our sister village is now joined to us by electric bonds!" read the jubilant headline of June 12, 1895. For trolley service that day had been extended from Matteawan to the village of Fishkill. The new line had been completed in only six weeks, with 10,500 chestnut ties laid over the 4.25-mile route. The new tracks ran along the left side of Fishkill Avenue up to Red Rock Hill in Glenham, through Glenham, and ended on Broad and Main Streets in Fishkill.

TROLLEY ON WASHINGTON STREET, C. 1910. The Citizens' Street Railway Company published the following safety rules for its motormen in 1892: "The gong must always be rung before turning on the current to start car; sound gong when approaching curves, crossings or the Ferry House; and when passing another car or when going through a crowded street. Do Not converse with passengers, except to answer a direct question. Slow down or stop when passing horses that are frightened or unruly."

MOTORMAN BEN ZOLESKI AND HIS TROLLEY, C. 1925. Since 1902, when the Mount Beacon Incline opened, the most popular destination by far on the trolley line was to the foot of the mountain. Many trolleys carried signs that read, "Dancing on Mt. Beacon, Wednesday and Saturday Evenings," to promote the resort and thereby increase their own business. The last leg of the 3-mile-trolley route to the mountain was full of jigsaw turns on narrow streets, a preamble to the adventurous ride to come up the mountain.

TROLLEYS AFTER SNOWSTORM, DONDERO BLOCK, MARCH 1914. The blizzard of March 1, 1914, disrupted service on Beacon's trolleys for almost three days. A heavy, wet snow fell on Sunday, March 1, bringing down power lines and suspending streetcar operations. By Monday, drifts of 4 and 5 feet covered the tracks to Fishkill. The plow car was ineffectual in the storm, so gangs of men had to shovel out the line. On Tuesday, after "almost superhuman effort," the trolley line to Fishkill was open.

TROLLEY IN SNOW ON EAST END OF MAIN STREET, 1914. Before the advent of the electric streetcar, getting about after a big snowfall presented a bleak prospect for the would-be traveler. Public transportation prior to 1892 came in the form of Weston's stagecoach line, which in winter was a slow, unreliable, and uncomfortable means of transport for the hapless rider. The electric trolley, on the other hand, was cheap, warm, and rarely foundered in the snow.

BIRNEY CAR ON MAIN STREET, C. 1928. By 1923, Beacon's trolley system was no longer showing a profit, so to boost revenues management petitioned to hike fares from a nickel to 7¢ a ride. Also in 1923, when the Newburgh trolley system switched to buses, Beacon upgraded its line by purchasing eight of Newburgh's newer trolleys, known as the "Birney Safety Cars." Improvements to the line notwithstanding, Beacon's trolleys would be replaced in 1930; the Birneys sold again to companies in Allentown, Pennsylvania; Springfield, Missouri; and Anniston, Alabama.

TROLLEY'S END OF THE LINE, C. 1930. On March 18, 1930, after 35 years of service, the trolleys made their final runs from Beacon to Fishkill. They were replaced by six buses the following day. "The trolleys had outlived their usefulness," explained James Meyer, the company president, "a bus made the same run faster and at a third less cost." Early on March 19, Samuel Delahay drove the first bus to Fishkill, making the run in record time. By April 30, bus service had replaced the trolley in Beacon.

Six

OF PRIDE AND PROGRESS

The 1870s were a turning point in the villages' history, as leaders invested in the community's institutions—and future—on a grand scale. The Matteawan School (1870), St. Luke's Church (1870), the Highland Hospital (1871), the Tioronda Bridge (1872), the Howland Library (1872), and the construction all along Main Street during the decade manifested, in bricks and mortar, a confidence in our future. These public buildings (and those that would follow) created a "community," and drew us together as a people.

THE HOWLAND CIRCULATING LIBRARY, C. 1872. In January of 1872, Gen. Joseph Howland gathered community leaders to form a library, and then commissioned his brother-in-law, famed architect Richard Morris Hunt, to design it. The doors opened on August 5, and within a year, the library could boast 2,914 volumes on its shelves. By 1895, the collection so overflowed that an upper-gallery was constructed. Nonetheless, the library eventually outgrew its gracious home, and after a century moved down Main Street to the larger quarters of a former 5&10 store.

ST. ANNA'S EPISCOPAL CHURCH, C. 1865. In 1833, one year after starting a Sunday school in their home, members of the Teller family donated a corner of their orchard for the construction of St. Anna's church. Consecrated on November 7, 1834, the house of worship was outgrown within 35 years. The property was sold, and the Matteawan Methodist Episcopal Church constructed in its stead at the corner of Main and Tioronda. The St. Anna's congregation changed not only its location but its name as well—building the larger St. Luke's Church in 1870.

ORIGINAL SPRINGFIELD BAPTIST CHURCH, C. 1950. The first black woman to become a Baptist minister in New York State, Rev. Mattie Cooper, began her first church in the former gas works at 16 Beekman Street in 1947. Born in Georgia in 1891 (the youngest of 21 children), Reverend Cooper christened the assembly in honor of her childhood church. She would later spend three years traveling Asia, Africa, and the Holy Land, spreading her mission. In 1972, she lead her own flock to its current home, located on a street since named in her honor. She died in 1990 at age 98.

ORIGINAL PRESBYTERIAN CHURCH, C. 1865. On Christmas Eve, 1832, 24 local residents met in a small room above the Matteawan Store to form the First Presbyterian Society of Matteawan. They soon set about building a fine Grecian-style edifice in which to worship—and paying a mortgage of $4,497. But within four decades, the congregation increased (even abolitionist Henry Ward Beecher became a summer parishioner) and the building had to be razed in 1870 because it had become too small to accommodate the burgeoning assembly.

SECOND PRESBYTERIAN CHURCH, 1872-1943. In the same year the Howland Library was constructed, the second Presbyterian church was completed by the same illustrious architect, Richard Morris Hunt. Both buildings benefited from the generosity of Hunt's brother-in-law, Gen. Joseph Howland. In 1914, a special election was held in which Beacon voters generously approved giving the church title to the once-public thoroughfare that separated it from its manse (rectory). The Gothic structure was destroyed by fire on February 17, 1943.

HIGHLAND HOSPITAL, 1871. Beacon's first hospital was a two-story frame house on Washington Street (now Russell Avenue). Donated to the community by General Howland in 1871, Highland Hospital served as the area's only hospital for 30 years. There were six rooms that could accommodate ten patients. The weekly charge was $6 for patients who could pay; those who could not were expected to assist the matron, if able, in light work and in caring for the sick.

HIGHLAND HOSPITAL, 1902-1960. More than one thousand people turned out to watch the cornerstone be laid for the new Highland Hospital on October 26, 1901. A time capsule containing silver coins, the first hospital report, and current newspapers was placed inside the stone. Miss Gertrude Balfe served as superintendent from 1918 through 1955—supervising the hospital, nursing the sick, and even canning the fruits and vegetables used in the kitchen. The new $1.4 million Highland Hospital would be dedicated on 10 acres off Delevan Avenue in 1960.

MATTEAWAN STATE HOSPITAL, C. 1920. On April 25, 1892, 60 prisoners from the asylum in Auburn arrived at the new State Asylum for the Criminally Insane (later Matteawan State Hospital and Fishkill Correctional Facility). The *Fishkill Standard* told of a large crowd gathered at the depot to see the chained prisoners, who arrived without incident—some carrying bird cages and baskets. Within a few short months, however, several escapes down drainpipes and into the village beyond caused enough concern to necessitate additional guards.

HAYING AT MATTEAWAN STATE HOSPITAL, C. 1920. Farm superintendent Charles A. Hancock supervises inmates as they gather hay, on the portion of the Matteawan State Hospital grounds that had been set aside for farming. In 1906, with the use of inmate labor to help grow crops, the hospital cut its yearly costs to maintain one patient to $181. In its early years the hospital farm had a greenhouse, a herd of cows, a piggery, a henhouse, and eight teams of horses—and, of course, a goal of self-sufficiency.

HUDSON-FULTON MONUMENT, c. 1920. Erected in 1909 at a cost of $850 (raised through public subscription), the Hudson-Fulton Monument once sat atop a horse fountain in the midst of our most prominent intersection, Bank Square. It is unclear if the statue depicts Diana (Goddess of the Hunt or Moon) or Hebe (Goddess of Youth). It is certain that she was designed to face the river in celebration of the 300th anniversary of Henry Hudson's voyage and the 100th anniversary of Robert Fulton's Clermont.

HUDSON-FULTON MONUMENT. When automobiles replaced horses, the need for public watering troughs disappeared, as nearly did the monument. In 1927, while Bank Square was being paved, Diana/Hebe was dismantled and laid to a rather inglorious rest among the city's barns. Then in 1931, the two hundred-member-strong West End Men's Community Club circulated a petition to resurrect the statue. A new home was readied on a small triangle of land on Verplanck Avenue—and Diana/Hebe was set once more to face the river.

FIRST LETTER CARRIERS IN BEACON. This photograph dates to August 1, 1908, taken on the occasion of the opening of free mail delivery to the Village of Fishkill Landing. This post office, officially called Fishkill-On-Hudson, was located on Bank Square. The new carriers dressed nattily in gray, were Fred Piano, Henry Annis, and Edmund Terwilliger. Their yearly salary was $600 and they earned it—walking their routes twice a day for morning and afternoon deliveries.

BEACON POST OFFICE NEAR COMPLETION, 1937. Constructed in 1936-37 by the federal Works Progress Administration, the Beacon Post Office epitomizes the fine craftsmanship and artistry that went into public buildings during the Depression. The stone for its foundation came from the old walls of the West Point Foundry in Cold Spring. The lobby's wall murals of local scenes were painted by WPA artists. In 1988 the Beacon Post Office was placed on the National Register of Historic Places.

DEDICATION CEREMONIES FOR MEMORIAL BUILDING, 1924. The turnout for the Memorial Day parade of 1924 was the largest in Beacon's history—two thousand marchers and ten thousand spectators filled the streets. What made the day a special occasion was the dedication ceremony that afternoon of the new World War Veterans' Memorial Building, built by the city as a monument to the living and dead soldiers from Beacon who served in the Great War.

WOLCOTT AVENUE BRIDGE, 1933. Beacon's unemployed of 1932 were hired for the Work Relief Project to build a new bridge over the Fishkill Creek at Wolcott Avenue. When architect Herbert Elton viewed the mountain and creek from that spot, he was inspired to design the bridge in an Egyptian motif. His idea took form with the bridge's massive buttresses, capped with a stepped detail. On the north face, he placed a winged sun disc, Egyptian symbol for the recurrence of life.

Seven
BACK TO SCHOOL

The story of our community's early schools unfolds within a one hundred-year timeline. It starts in 1815, when Fishkill Landing organizes the area's first school district, and ends in 1915, when the new city of Beacon decides to build a central high school. The story of our schools is one of faces familiar and forgotten, of settings now lost or recast, and of a time unlike ours but of people just like us.

GIRLS OF "D" PRIMARY DEPARTMENT, MATTEAWAN UNION SCHOOL, NOVEMBER 7, 1888. Most children growing up in the latter part of the 19th century did not have the chance to finish school. The compulsory schooling laws of the time simply were not enforced, and after some grammar school, children either went to work or helped at home. Of the 60 girls who posed in this picture, only five would graduate from Matteawan High School's Class of 1897. No male student received a diploma that year.

TIORONDA SCHOOL, c. 1875. Miles apart from all other early schools in our history stands the former Tioronda School. Designed by renowned architect Frederick Clarke Withers, the building is unexpectedly churchly in appearance—and, in fact, it was once used as a chapel. Built in 1865, it is our oldest schoolhouse extant. Its long history even includes hospital duty: during the Great Flu Epidemic of 1918 the Red Cross used the school as an emergency hospital to treat the overflow of Beacon's sick.

PRINCIPAL HAIGHT AND STUDENTS, TIORONDA SCHOOL, C. 1886. Professor Eugene Haight's career profile was that of any archetypal dedicated teacher. He was the principal of Tioronda School from 1886 to 1916, a record of longevity in one place unmatched by any educator. When the school board forced him to retire, so they could hire a woman at lesser salary, two generations of his students—including 12 who were now teachers—professed their admiration for him. Haight resigned quietly with a $50-a-month pension.

ACADEMY SCHOOL, C. 1880S. The origins of public education in our community trace back to a small side street off South Avenue in Fishkill Landing in the year 1826. There, in the form of a modest wood-frame schoolhouse, built at a cost of $250, public schooling began. This original Academy Street School would be replaced in 1857 by a brick structure with its separate "colored annex." In 1891, the Dutchess Tool Company occupied the site when the new South Avenue School opened down the road.

PRINCIPAL EGBERT LEWIS AND STAFF, ACADEMY STREET SCHOOL, C. 1888. Teaching was the one profession open to women in the 19th century. The job entailed working with oversized classes, at a poor salary, under male supervision. An agreement of employment was that you must remain single—marriage for women meant dismissal, a rule in effect in Beacon until the 1930s. One applicant's recommendation sums up what was expected: "She is tall, strong, healthy in appearance, understands herself well, and can manage any school in the country."

MATTEAWAN SCHOOL, LOOKING FROM SPRING STREET, C. 1880S. Matteawan after the Civil War was a village prosperous with burgeoning factories and swelled with a population double that of Fishkill Landing. Yet for its children there was no centralized public school, only two small houses—one on Masters Place, one on DePuyster Avenue—served as classrooms. But growth and prosperity were the proper mix for better schooling, and in 1870 the Matteawan Union School opened. It would serve the community for the next 83 years.

MATTEAWAN SCHOOL, C. 1890. The 19th-century classroom could be a warm, bright place to learn, like this Matteawan schoolroom with its potbelly stove and wall of windows. Or conditions could be wretched. In 1843 the children of Matteawan attended school in the basement of the Presbyterian church. When it rained, the basement flooded and frogs moved in under the floorboards. Teachers found it hard to teach because of the damp, the dark, and the croaking of frogs.

MISS NETTIE DELONG'S SECOND GRADE CLASS, MATTEAWAN SCHOOL, FEBRUARY 1911. If we could observe any schoolroom before 1890, most likely we would find an austere dreary atmosphere more befitting a factory workplace. Progressive reform at the turn of the century, however, changed old attitudes about teaching: classrooms thereafter were to be bright, homey, and open to learning. Miss DeLong's classroom, with its vase of pussywillows and bulletin board of children's cutouts, reflects the new theory that school should be a friendly place.

SPRING STREET SCHOOL BURNS, 1954. After 83 years in session, the old Spring Street School was replaced by the new James V. Forrestal School. The old school bell, someone suggested, should be salvaged and preserved at the new school, a legacy from older generations to the young. In 1953, a "Save Our Bell" campaign by alumni raised money to restore the bell and place it in Forrestal's schoolyard. Just in time, too: Spring Street School was destroyed by fire on August 26, 1954.

PUBLIC SCHOOL OF FISHKILL LANDING, C. 1890S. The Fishkill-on-Hudson Union School was the antecedent of today's South Avenue School. When it opened in 1891, there were 438 students enrolled in the primary, grammar, and academic departments. The school's syllabus spells out a sobering fact of the times: "Inasmuch as many of our boys and girls never enter high school, special attention is given to work in the grammar department." Fire destroyed the school in 1928.

RUINS OF SOUTH AVENUE SCHOOL, 1928. "The South Avenue School is on Fire!"—that shout heard around town on the evening of January 2, 1928, brought people out to see one of Beacon's most spectacular fires. By night's end, the school was a total loss, its five hundred pupils now forced to attend afternoon sessions at Spring Street School. It was a happy arrangement for some: grades one through three got to ride the trolley across town to school all year.

SARGENT INDUSTRIAL SCHOOL FOR GIRLS, C. 1900. The Sargent Industrial School, in operation from 1891 to 1918, was one of the first private schools to teach and train girls in home economics. Aimee Sargent (insert), whose husband owned the estate "Wodenethe," founded the school so young girls might learn homemaking as a science and thereby become better servants and housewives. The school was located on Schenck Avenue, and its concept proved popular, for nearly ten thousand girls enrolled in its programs.

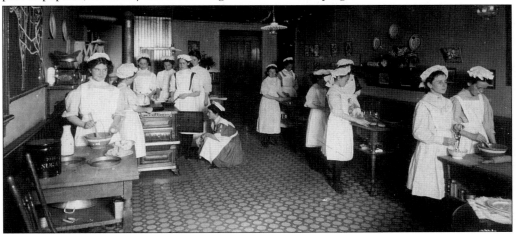

COOKING CLASS, SARGENT INDUSTRIAL SCHOOL, C. 1915. Sargent school students were taught the domestic sciences—cooking, sewing, dressmaking, laundry work, and gardening. No tuition was charged, but two unexcused absences meant automatic dismissal. As the school's reputation in the community grew, so did the waiting list for admission. But the school closed, in accordance with Mrs. Sargent's wishes, with her death in 1918. Ironically, that had been its most successful year, with 809 students enrolled.

DeGarmo Institute, c. 1899. The succession of four private boarding schools—the Mount Beacon Academy, the DeGarmo Institute, the Mount Beacon Military Academy, and the Caswell Academy—once occupied a three-story brick building on Rombout Avenue during the years 1885 to 1920. Of these, Professor James DeGarmo's school achieved nationwide recognition. Male students from across America and the world came to the institute for its college preparatory courses. The school closed in 1899 with DeGarmo's death, and was replaced by a military academy.

Matteawan High School Football Team, 1911. High school football in its early days here was a Spartan sport. Henry Forrestal, a member of the Matteawan team, recalled: "We had no money, no equipment. Most of the boys worked after school, so we had to scrimmage by moonlight. We all chipped in and paid for the balls and having goal posts put in the field." From this scrappy group came at least one player of quality—Gordon "Rip" Flannery, a 1913 Matteawan graduate who went on to become an All-American in football at Syracuse University.

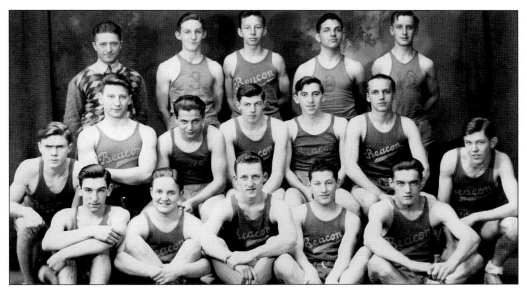

BEACON HIGH BASKETBALL TEAM, 1937. Beacon is the hometown of the man who changed how college basketball is played. Edward Steitz (seated at far left), who coached at Springfield College, was an authority on basketball rules. As a member of the NCAA rules committee, he introduced (among other changes), the three-point shot and the 45-second shot clock to college play. For his contributions to the sport, Steitz was elected to the Basketball Hall of Fame in 1984.

COACH HAMM AND BEACON HIGH SCHOOL TRACK TEAM, 1937. Coach William Hamm was the physical education instructor at Beacon High from 1932 through the 1950s, coaching basketball, baseball, and track. Many of the members of the track team in this photograph were soon to serve in World War II, including Roscoe Vaughn Jr. (first row, second from left). In 1944, Vaughn was killed in action in North Africa, the first African American from Beacon to die in the war.

MATTEAWAN HIGH SCHOOL GRADUATING CLASS, 1905. Most children going to school at the beginning of the 20th century would not complete high school. Early graduating classes were small; the combined graduating classes of Matteawan and Fishkill Landing High Schools were usually comprised of ten students or less. The small group who did receive diplomas were predominantly female and often from the more prosperous families of the community. Most children of that era, especially males, left school early to go to work.

BEACON JUNIOR HIGH SCHOOL GRADUATING CLASS, 1918. In February of 1916, the new $60,000 high school on Fishkill Avenue first opened its doors to former students of Matteawan and Fishkill-on-Hudson schools, thus completing the final step in officially unifying the two villages into the new city of Beacon. That June, 20 members of the class of 1916 became the first graduates of Beacon High School. The new building housed grades 7 through 12, including the latest in educational reform, a junior high school.

Eight

WELCOME HOME

Nestled at the foot of Mount Beacon and poised at the northern gate of the Hudson Highlands, the villages became ideal locations for Hudson River estates. Impressive houses—several designed by the world's foremost architects—graced the two communities. "(T)he fact should not be lost sight of that this town offers the double attraction of unsurpassed facilities for business and a situation for building up a beautiful home with surroundings in which both nature and art combine in making all that is desirable," local leaders wrote in 1889. From mountain's slope to river's edge, breathtaking scenery drew the discriminating settler.

MADAM BRETT HOMESTEAD, C. 1900. Though the visitors of today are most likely to be schoolchildren who come to tour the oldest building in Dutchess County, Washington and Lafayette once danced the minuet with Brett descendants in the main drawing room of the Madam Brett Homestead. The original portion was built in about 1709 by Roger and Catheryna Rombout Brett. Notable features of the Dutch-style house include handmade scalloped shingles, a native stone foundation, and hand-hewn beams. In 1954, the house was to be razed for a supermarket when the Melzingah Chapter of the DAR enlisted the support of the community in raising $14,000 to purchase it.

DePeyster House, c. 1925. Abraham DePeyster was Madam Brett's step-nephew and a successful New York City merchant who took title to 300 acres of her property in 1743. He is believed to have constructed this handsome country estate (including a gambrel roof, six-pane window glass, 10-foot ceilings, and a central hall staircase) in the mid-1700s. But the banks of the Fishkill Creek later invited the nearby construction of a factory. And in 1954 (the same year the Brett house was saved), the home was razed to expand the Atlas Fibers complex.

Chrystie House. This Federal-style residence, extant on South Avenue, was originally located across the street, but was moved in 1927 when encroaching brickyards undermined its foundation. The home, once called Castagna, was built in 1821 and through a twist of fate, became the site of a small piece of American history. Col. William Few, who signed our nation's Constitution on behalf of the State of Georgia, died in the home while visiting his daughter, wife of Maj. Albert Chrystie, in 1828.

ROSENEATH. Built in 1856 by a U.S. Navy lieutenant, Roseneath is most commonly associated with 19th-century industrialist Charles Wolcott. Sadly, the family's estate was abandoned and in ruin before being razed by an arsonist in 1991. Writing of Roseneath in the 1870s, Henry Sargent noted: "Mr. Wolcott has every attribute of a well-kept country place—. . . an English flower garden; a most successful vegetable garden; . . . the most charming views, and no apparent boundary but river and mountain."

THE WOLCOTTS. Charles Wolcott held an interest in the New York Rubber Company. His grandfather had signed the Declaration of Independence and won fame as the man who had the leaden statue of King George III taken down, melted, and made into bullets for American soldiers. Wolcott's daughter, Katherine Wolcott Verplanck, was a dedicated community volunteer: serving on the Board of Education, administering the local Red Cross Chapter during World War I, and founding the Melzingah Chapter of the DAR.

NORTH SHORE AT DENNING'S POINT, C. 1865. Presqu'ile, "almost an island," was the 45-acre estate of the Dennings from 1821 until 1894. Emily Denning Van Rensselaer described hers as a "charming life," and recollected that the family "had a sailboat anchored off our dock, and rowboats and a barge to take ourselves and friends to and from Newburgh." A border of magnificent trees surrounded Presqu'ile, including the pair of "Washington Oaks" where George Washington had landed when crossing from his Newburgh headquarters.

PRESQU'ILE, C. 1865. The heirs of Gulian Verplanck built the first home on Denning's Point; it was later modified to Greek Revival style. Emily Denning VanRensselaer (insert) recalled, "The house was always filled with guests from the beginning to the end of season . . . Our stable was always filled with horses, and large riding and driving parties would scour the country or ascend the Beacon." Among the distinguished visitors to stay at Presqu'ile were Pres. Martin Van Buren, en route to his inauguration, and Millard Fillmore.

WODENETHE, THE SARGENT ESTATE, C. 1870. "The most beautiful place in the United States," was one leading magazine's description of "Wodenethe." "The finest specimen of modern landscape gardening in America," said another. For 40 years, it was the labor of love of Henry Winthrop Sargent, who considered himself an artist painting—not with oils on canvas, but with the colors of nature on a breathtaking Hudson River landscape. So bright was the palette, one visitor exclaimed, "You fancy yourself gazing on the richest Brussels carpet ever made."

DIANNA GARDEN, C. 1870. An Anglophile with an affinity for English Gardens, Sargent christened his estate with the words for "god of the woods" and "promontory." A friend and apt student of Andrew Jackson Downing, Sargent had a genius for selecting and cultivating plants. He spent decades collecting trees, shrubs, and flowers from throughout the world for his magnificent country estate—experimenting, sometimes without success, in selecting species he thought might grow in the variable weather of the Hudson Valley.

SARGENT, THE GARDENER AS ARTIST, C. 1870. Sargent (insert), who was born in Boston and maintained a lifelong city residence there, devoted much of his adult life to his gardening masterpiece, Wodenethe. Along the way, he created one of the great exotic plant collections in America. Near the end of his life, Sargent told a visiting reporter, "I have been painting a picture," he said as he strolled through the grounds, "and the finishing touches are still to be given."

"THE FINISHING TOUCHES," c. 1870. Wodenethe, which was remodeled by noted architect Calvert Vaux, passed to Sargent's son Winthrop, in 1882. The estate remained within the family for 40 more years, and was eventually acquired by the Craig House properties. In 1955, builders lotted out the "Wodenethe Drive" development over its once-famous acres; and Wodenethe was razed to make way for the popular ranch houses of the era. But amid the suburban backyards of today, still stand some of Sargent's renowned trees—silent witnesses to the glory of yesterday.

GENERAL JOSEPH AND ELIZABETH WOOLSEY HOWLAND. Owners of the beautiful estate "Tioronda," the Howlands were perhaps our city's most important benefactors in the second half of the 19th century. After the Civil War, in which both husband and wife served with distinction—he with the 16th New York, she as a nurse in the U.S. Sanitary Commission—the Howlands' gifts to our community included the Tioronda School, the first Highland Hospital, the First Presbyterian Church, and the Howland Library.

TIORONDA. Famed architect Frederick Clark Withers completed the Howlands' home in 1861, amidst a scenic 97-acre mountainside property. Originally named "Glenhurst," the Howlands later found the Native American word "Tioronda" (meaning the 'meeting of the waters') more to their liking. All of the furniture at the estate was made to order. The house was steam-heated and lighted by gas, produced in a brick gashouse on the property.

MUSIC ROOM ADDITION. The Howlands' brother-in-law, Richard Morris Hunt, designed the music wing addition to Tioronda in 1873, and its massive pipe organ still operates. After General Howland's death, Mrs. Howland offered Tioronda to village officials for a village hall and park, but they refused. The home eventually became Craig House Hospital, a private facility with exclusive amenities that once included a nine-hole golf course, an indoor swimming pool, and the fine original library.

EUSTATIA. Frederick Clark Withers also designed this fine home, built in 1865 for Judge John Monell and his wife, Caroline DeWindt Downing (the widow of Andrew Jackson Downing and Withers's sister-in-law). Now listed on the National Register of Historic Places, the estate was named for the West Indies island from which the DeWindts had emigrated. Still a private residence at the intersection of Monell and Lafayette Avenues, the home's architectural integrity has been undermined by two serious fires.

MONTE ALLEGRO. "A charming example of the interesting residences for which this picturesque section is noted," said *Country Homes* magazine of this home in 1923. The house, situated on the 12 acres of today's Forrestal Heights, was once owned by Dr. Guernsey of New York City and later owned by Latourette Brinckerhoff. It featured seven fireplaces, a music room, and French windows that opened to the front porch. The home was converted into four apartments by the 1960s, and demolished during Urban Renewal.

VAN HOUTEN HOUSE. This five-story brick estate, built for Frank Van Houten (president of Dutchess Tool Company), included a top-floor billiard room. In 1922, the home was valued at the then-enormous sum of $17,500. From 1943 through 1959, it was owned by Benjamin Roosa, whose son fondly recalls keeping a horse and other animals on the property. All that remains is the driveway, an inauspicious strip of blacktop stretching from today's Route 9D to the rear of the Colonial Springs condominiums, current occupants of this site.

EDGEWATER. This fine Victorian was the home of Lewis Tompkins, who was born in Greene County in 1836 and settled in Matteawan in the 1860s. In 1872, he sold nearly all of his business interests to spend a year abroad, where he studied that continent's factory systems. Upon his return, he established Dutchess Hat Works and later, the Tioronda Hat Works. He is credited as the man most responsible for making Beacon the "Hat Capital of New York State."

AINSWORTH HOME, C. 1900. Alan Ainsworth (seated) was an English immigrant who arrived in Beacon in the 1860s to find work in the local hat factories. Organist and choirmaster at St. Luke's Church, he constructed the family home at 88 Prospect Street. Young Harry Ainsworth, seated at his father's feet, would later own the Long Dock Coal Company. Harry's daughter, Vivian Ainsworth Bolton, became an early Beacon preservationist and received the Beacon Historical Society's first Howland Award for Historic Preservation in 1994.

RIVERVIEW SANATORIUM. From 1904 until 1914, Dr. James R. Bolton operated a "select private home for nervous invalids" at this house on Ferry Street. An advertisement for the facility noted "all approved methods of treatment used, including diet, baths, massage, and electricity." The home may have been built by Milo Sage, president of the Fishkill Landing Machine Company. In time, it would sadly share the same fate of so many other fine homes of yesterday: conversion to apartments before eventual demolition.

KNEVELS ESTATE, C. 1930. This home on South Avenue was one of three on the property owned by the Knevels family, according to an 1876 map. Charles Fisher, who manufactured fine toys in a Main Street building, lived here with his family from 1924 until 1933. But when the Great Depression devastated the toy industry, Fisher was forced to sell the house and auction its contents. The home was all but lost too—when it was incorporated into the west wing of the St. Lawrence Seminary in the 1930s.

ROTHERY ESTATE. With its mansard roof and wrap-around porch of yesterday, this home is impossible to recognize today—for it was incorporated into the Elks Club after the Beacon BPOE purchased the property in 1927. William Rothery's homestead was called "Fairview." William had been born in Matteawan in 1834, his father John having arrived from England in 1828. Coincidentally, the Schenck Avenue home of William's brother John would also evolve into an alternate use, becoming the Sargent Industrial School.

SOUTH STREET APARTMENTS. When constructed about 1890, these brick rowhouses were likely our first buildings built exclusively as "apartments." Also likely to have been a comparatively upscale address, they were surely built to help meet the housing demand resulting from the boom at local hat factories (which reached their zenith in the 1890s). In 1890, the federal census recorded 5,961 people in Matteawan and a population of 4,296 in Fishkill Landing; in contrast, a total of just 682 residents was living in the village of Fishkill.

WOLCOTT AVENUE HOMES, 1913. Wolcott Avenue, with its bed of dirt and row of trees, could have been the welcoming entrance to any small community at the time of the city's formation in 1913. A March tornado that year, which felled this tree, was one of the worst in local memory. Many roofs, including those of the Tioronda Hat Shop and the New York Rubber Company, were pulled off in the narrow path of the storm, which also leveled outbuildings and chimneys in its wake.

DUTCHESS TERRACE HOMES. To encourage hat shop employees to settle here, Lewis Tompkins bought and developed land near his first factory, and laid out a series of streets with homes for his workers. Today the streets of northwest Beacon, including Tompkins, Mackin, and Lafayette Avenues; Dutchess Terrace; and West Church Street, trace their origin to Tompkins' plan for a workers' community. Also included was Ralph Street, which was named for his son, who would one day be appointed postmaster of Fishkill-on-Hudson by Pres. Theodore Roosevelt.

Nine

SERVICE TO OUR NATION, OUR NEIGHBORS

Here are the men and women who have served their country and their community with honor and sacrifice. The line of march of those who have answered the call to duty stretches back beyond the Civil War. For generations we, as a community, have cheered on that long parade, justly proud that from Beacon have come such worthy and unselfish men and women.

CIVIL WAR VETERANS, 1916. They were the young men who had answered their country's call to preserve the Union. They were veterans of battles like Gettysburg and the Wilderness. Some had seen Lincoln, Grant, and Lee. A few had experienced the worst hellholes of the war—places like Libby Prison and Andersonville. Fifty years after the war, their number diminished by time, the local chapter of the Grand Army of the Republic gathered for what would be a final group portrait.

MAJOR JOHN HENRY AND ELIZABETH DOUGHTY, 1864. Assistant Surgeon U.S. Volunteers Major Doughty, M.D., and his wife, Elizabeth, pose for their wedding portrait. Dr. Doughty soon returned to duty as post surgeon at a North Carolina base. There he treated and saved soldiers with severe malaria. In 1866, the Doughtys settled in Matteawan, where he practiced medicine for the next 40 years. Their daughter Phebe became one of the area's first female physicians.

CIVIL WAR MONUMENT, 1900. Memorial Days of yesteryear would find Beacon's Civil War veterans convening at the Soldiers and Sailors Monument in Fairview Cemetery to honor their fallen comrades. In 1903, in a ceremony with patriotic songs and cannons firing, the statue of a soldier—placed atop the original monument—was unveiled. Later, this soldier would fall to vandals, but would be replaced and restored by the Beacon Historical Society in 1989.

OLD SOLDIERS ON PARADE, C. 1915. Imagine the thrill of the young spectators on that long ago Memorial Day as they watched the old soldiers in blue march by on East Main Street. To think, some of these old men had fought the Army of Northern Virginia, against Lee and Jackson! The final salutes were exchanged in 1933, when Daniel Barrett, Beacon's last Civil War vet, died at the age of 87. Benjamin Merritt of Chelsea, the last member of Beacon's GAR, died in 1937.

GAR VETERANS IN COLUMBUS DAY PARADE, 1916. A highlight of the big parade day events in Beacon before World War I was the appearance of the Grand Army of the Republic. Howland Post 48, the official title of the local chapter of the GAR, was formed in Matteawan in 1870. Named after local resident and Civil War Gen. Joseph Howland, the veterans' group was active in Beacon for 60 years, with as many as 230 members on its roll call.

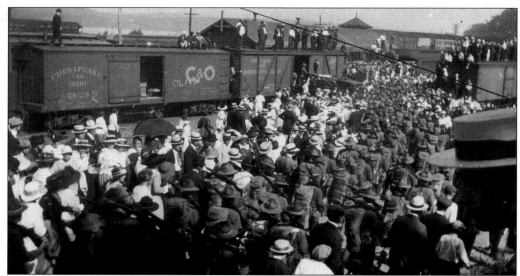

SEEING OFF SOLDIERS FROM NEWBURGH'S COMPANY L AT BEACON TRAIN STATION, 1917. During the First World War, 56 men from Beacon served in Newburgh's Company L, 107th Infantry. Of that group, six Beacon soldiers lost their lives in battle: William B. Wilson (the first Beacon boy to be killed in the war), John F. Bump, and Fred A. Garrison were killed in action in France. George Delahay, Thomas B. Carroll, and Charles Haight died in hospitals from their wounds.

BEACON RED CROSS VOLUNTEERS IN FRONT OF KNIGHTS OF COLUMBUS HALL, 1918. With needles, thread, and yarn the female members of the Town of Fishkill branch of the American Red Cross sewed and knitted their part in the war effort during World War I. The group met Monday and Thursday afternoons in rooms of the Knights of Columbus Hall on Main Street. Their assignment from the Red Cross was to make surgical dressings and garments desperately needed in French military hospitals during the summer offensives of 1918.

WORLD WAR I PARADE, 1919. The Great War, the Armistice, and the return of our victorious soldiers were cause for great celebrations and parades in Beacon. The grandest celebration of all had come on the evening of the announcement of the Armistice. "By 7 o'clock that night," the *Beacon News* reported, "Main Street was one mass of humanity from the ferry terminal to the foot of the mountain. The jubilant crowd marched to Bank Square, then countermarched back to Fountain Square in their euphoria over the Allies' victory."

"WELCOME HOME" PARADE FOR BEACON SOLDIERS, 1919. On June 14, 1919, Main Street was the setting for a huge patriotic parade to welcome home the local soldiers and sailors returning from the war. All told, about 570 Beacon boys had served in the Great War, with 13 giving their lives. Those who died are the following: John Bump, Thomas Carroll, George Delahay, George Deverson, Gordon Diecke, Fred Garrison, Francis Murphy, Austin Robinson, Pasquale Sales, George Stafford, James Tomlins, Frank Van Houten, and William Wilson.

ELKS CLUB RECEPTION FOR DRAFTEES, 1942. For many draftees from Beacon, the memory of the last happy hours before they reported for active duty would be the send-off ceremony given them at the Elks club. There the young men would be treated to a luncheon served by Red Cross volunteers and the American Legion Auxiliary. After the lunch and the patriotic speeches, the draftees marched in a parade to the railroad station, cheered on by well wishers all along Main Street.

WORLD WAR II HONOR ROLL AT MEMORIAL HALL, 1943. Beacon was the first city in the Hudson Valley to erect an honor roll, a large board of names listing all the local men serving in the U.S. Armed Forces in World War II. By the end of the war, the honor roll was expanded to include more than 1,700 names. And of that number, 67 had hand-painted gold stars beside them, signifying those men who had made the highest sacrifice.

FRANCIS PEATTIE, 1918-1943. Lt. Frank Peattie, a bombardier on a B-17, and the first Beaconite in the war to earn a Silver Star, was killed June 26, 1943, on a bombing raid over New Guinea. The lone survivor of his crew, Jose Holguin, returned to the crash site three times after the war trying to recover his buddies' remains. In 1983, Holguin discovered that Peattie and four others were buried in unmarked graves in Hawaii. Beacon's missing hero, Frank Peattie, was returned home and given a full-military burial in 1985.

ROBERT RESEK, 1943. Sgt. Bob Resek of Beacon was killed in action near the German border. President Roosevelt's office sent his family this message of condolence: "In grateful memory of Sergeant Robert Resek, who died in the service of his country in the European Area, November 20, 1944. He stands in the unbroken line of patriots who have dared to die so that freedom might live and grow and increase its blessing. Freedom lives, and through it, he lives—in a way that humbles the undertakings of most men."

PHIL AND LILLIAN COMEAU, 1942. The dreaded news came by telegram: MRS LILLIAN COMEAU I REGRET TO INFORM YOU YOUR HUSBAND STAFF SGT PHILBERT COMEAU MISSING IN ACTION OVER KASSEL GERMANY. In 1943, Phil Comeau of Beacon was captured in Holland after bailing out of his stricken B-17. For months after, his wife had no news of his fate until a postcard arrived from a German prison camp: "Everything is O.K. Keep your chin up. Hope to see you soon. Love, Phil."

ELKS CLUB RECEPTION FOR AVIATION CADETS, 1942. Among the Beacon aviation cadets to complete the program was Lt. John Briggs, a 1939 graduate of Beacon High School. Briggs was a bombardier assigned to the 364th Squadron of the 305th Bomb Group based in England. In 1943, while flying missions over Germany, Briggs earned the Air Medal with three Oak Leaf Clusters and the Distinguished Service Medal for gallantry and courage in the face of tremendous opposition. He was killed on a raid over Schweinfurt in 1944.

"E" Award Ceremony at New York Rubber, 1943. One of Beacon's leading defense plants during World War II was the New York Rubber Corporation, which produced life preservers, rafts, and other rubber goods for the war effort. On October 18, 1943, in a ceremony at the factory, Under Secretary of the Navy and Beacon native James Forrestal (seated, behind the podium, wearing a hat) presented the Army-Navy "E" Production Award to the company for its outstanding production of war materials.

Female Workers at New York Rubber Company, 1943. After Pearl Harbor, a woman's place no longer was at home but in the workplace. In Beacon, hundreds of women joined the workforce in local factories to help the war effort. At New York Rubber five hundred new workers—mostly women—worked six-day weeks making life rafts. At Bobrich, seven hundred employees made electrically heated flying suits. And at Aero-Leather Clothing, women assembled leather jackets and aviator suits for the Army Air Forces.

FISHKILL LANDING POLICE FORCE, C. 1905. Unfortunately, few details are known of the villages' early police departments. The new city's force of ten men was housed in the Matteawan station and was led by Chief Theodore Moith. That first city squad also included John O'G. Middleton (far left), who had been hired as an officer within the Fishkill Landing Police force on April 20, 1891. That village's police station on Beekman Street continued in use as a substation for the combined city department for many years.

OFFICER CHARLES LUCY, C. 1920. Beacon's only police officer to be killed in the line of duty was Charles Lucy, who died on August 14, 1922. Wellington White, distraught over the unrelated death of his own father, shot the responding officer as he climbed the family's North Street porch. In a vigilante cry for justice, hundreds of armed townspeople responded to the neighborhood and began firing at the house. An hour later, White was shot through a window. Thousands attended Lucy's funeral, paying final tribute to Beacon's Badge #16.

OFFICERS KIRKUP AND VAN PELT, CHIEF JESSE DINGEE, 1935. In November 1935, Chief Dingee (Beacon's longest-running chief, 1926-1957) and his men packed up and moved to Beacon Engine's firehouse—which would serve as a temporary lockup while the old Matteawan jail was renovated as a WPA project. Three cage-cells were transferred and a temporary city courtroom and headquarters established. A year and $24,294 later, the renovated station awaited—along with good news for patrolmen: legislation had reduced their work shifts from 12 to eight hours.

BEACON POLICE DEPARTMENT, 1936. Mayor Irving Justus and Chief Dingee pose front and center with Beacon's finest. Appointed to the new city's force in 1913, Joseph Dardis (far right) had been originally hired as an officer in the Matteawan Police Department in 1910. During World War II's manpower shortage, Dardis postponed retirement to continue service to the city. In 1944, at age 72, after quelling a disturbance, he returned to the station house and suffered a fatal heart attack.

APPARATUS OF MATTEAWAN FIRE DEPARTMENT, BEACON ENGINE COMPANY. Eleven members founded Beacon Engine Company in August 1886, and their $5,000 firehouse was constructed three years later. A hand engine, previously used by the disbanded Protection Engine Company, became their first piece of equipment. On March 6, 1893, the governing ordinance of the Matteawan Fire Department was issued by the village trustees; it decreed that men older than 18 years who lived in the village were eligible for membership, providing they were of "good moral character."

WASHING HORSE-DRAWN WAGON AT TOMPKINS HOSE COMPANY, C. 1900. Fishkill Landing had been without any fire protection since 1881, when the Excelsior and Engine #1 units had disbanded. In 1886, 30 charter members formed a new company, and eight years after his death, chose to name it Lewis Tompkins Hose Company in honor of the well-respected community businessman and benefactor. The company's three-story firehouse—complete with tower and fire bell—was built a year later.

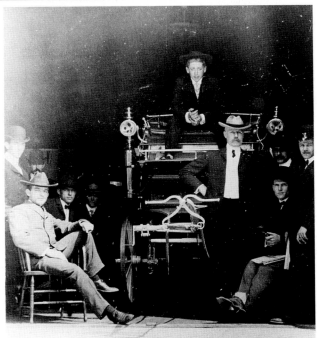

ABOVE, RACING TO A FIRE, C. 1915. RIGHT, TOMPKINS HOSE MEMBERS, 1910. Reflecting in 1921 on the earlier formation of our fire companies, local publisher Morgan Hoyt wrote, "The little band of humble villagers who long ago assembled to organize a fire department for the protection of our homes, our property, and for the safety of the community in which they dwelt were no less public benefactors than were the philanthropist, the statesman, or the solider, each of whom in their distinctive sphere, contributed much to the welfare of mankind."

"Ben," the Fire Horse, c. 1910. The first to every fire, standing out with his white mane and regal bearing, he was the most revered and popular member of the fire department. He was "Ben," the great white steed of the Lewis Tompkins Hose Company, who pulled their apparatus from 1903 to 1918. More than just a fire horse though, Ben became the town pet and the department's most visible representative. In 1918, he was retired to pasture, replaced by a shiny, red Ahrens Fox motorized truck.

Fire Apparatus of Lewis Tompkins Hose Company, Fishkill–on–Hudson, N. Y.

FIRST MOTORIZED APPARATUS, 1912. The installation of water mains greatly improved the fire department's ability to protect lives and property, but also, of course, necessitated modern firefighting equipment. And so, Beacon Engine's shiny, new-fangled Webb automotive apparatus arrived in 1912, replacing a chemical and hose wagon in use since 1904. Its first driver was Bob McCarroll, who was paid $750 a year for the 24-hour-a-day job. In 1924, the firehouse was expanded to make way for yet a more advanced apparatus.

FIRE ENGINES COLLIDE, C. 1920. Could the friendly rivalry to be the first company arriving at the fire scene have contributed to this mishap? Rounding the Fishkill Avenue bend near Blackburn Avenue, Beacon Engine Company and Mase Hook and Ladder met quite literally by accident—and neither ever quite made it to the fire. Not permanently damaged, the Mase apparatus is a 1915 Seagrave that would continue on in steadfast service to the city and its residents until 1940.

MASE HOOK AND LADDER, C. 1913. Formed in 1887, Mase's had no equipment until 1895, when the village purchased a gig with wheels so the members could roll ladders to a fire. Their supplies were stored in a shed behind the village hall. By 1897, the company had its first official quarters at the corner of Main and Schenck and there was stored its first hand- and horse-drawn ladder truck in 1898. In 1911, a handsome and permanent new home was built across the street.

J. ROBERT CRAMER, PRESIDENT, TOMPKINS HOSE. Despite stinging cold, the 2:15 a.m. alarm of fire at the Town Tavern had brought firefighters clamoring to 144-146 Main Street that January morning in 1955. Yet theirs would be a slow march down Main Street just days later, as members trailed an engine carrying the flag-draped coffin of a fallen comrade. Pharmacist and volunteer fireman Bobby Cramer had died alone in the smoke-filled bedroom of the building's second-floor apartment—his attempt to rescue victims instead resulting in his own tragic death.

Ten

ORDINARY PEOPLE, EVERYDAY LIVES

Wars, politics, great leaders, and turning-point events are the usual focus of historical study. Of equal importance in appreciating our past, however, is the story of ordinary people and their everyday lives. How were their Sundays and weekday evenings spent? What groups did they join, what entertainment did they enjoy? What made them happy? What made them proud? When we discover what was truly important to our great-grandmothers and grandfathers, we usually find out what matters to us as well.

OUT FOR A SUNDAY DRIVE, 1892. The hitching post and an unpaved Main Street denote the simpler times of horse-and-buggy days, as Mary Rothery Jackson and her daughter Veda Louise sit in their carriage in front of the Jackson home on Main Street in Matteawan. Veda, whose grandfather was William Jackson (the respected carriage-maker in town), later fondly recalled these carriage rides on summer Sunday afternoons, as well as sleigh rides in winter with horse and cutter on a snow-packed Main Street.

St. Joachim's Dramatics Society, c. 1886. Local church groups, such as the St. Joachim's Literary and Dramatics Society, often were the mainstays of culture in 19th-century village life. The St. Joachim's club offered "domestic and spectacular plays by home talent exclusively." Their first production of the 1886 season was the melodrama *The Social Glass*, performed at the Dibble Opera House, admission—25¢.

Baptism in the Hudson, 1897. The prosperous brick-making industry once drew hundreds of black laborers from the South each spring, and the Star Mission was founded in Fishkill Landing to meet the spiritual needs of these migratory workers. In May 1897, the mission held an open-air religious meeting by the river, and a crowd of 1,500 witnessed the baptism of ten converts in the Hudson. The practice would continue until the 1960s, when it was stopped by the City due to concerns that the river had become too polluted.

RUF FAMILY PORTRAIT, C. 1900.
Ludwig Ruf was born in Baden, Germany, in 1857 and immigrated to America in 1880, settling in Fishkill Landing to find work in the local brickyards. He and his wife, Christina, who was also born in Germany, built a house on Wilkes Street and maintained a farm (between Wilkes and Maple Streets) which supplied produce to local stores. Their grandson, Ludwig Ruf, would become the first president of the Beacon Historical Society at its formation in 1976.

GIORDANO FAMILY, C. 1915. The Giordano family arrived in the brand-new city of Beacon in 1913, when Vincent found work at the Groveville Textile Mill. He had come to America in 1905 from Potenza, Italy, and had sent for his family to join him in Brooklyn two years later. With wife Magdoline, and a family that eventually grew to include ten children, he first moved into the "mud huts" factory housing at Groveville. There the family lived the new American Dream for 16 years before moving across the creek to Liberty Street in 1929.

MATTEAWAN MANNERCHOR ("MALE CHORUS"), C. 1900. Choral groups were in vogue at the beginning of the 20th century in the twin villages, and everyone, it seems, had a song to be sung and a voice to be heard. In 1904 alone, four new singing groups emerged: St. Luke's Choral Society, the Choral Society of Sargent Industrial School, the Presbyterian Church Choir, and the Matteawan Choral Society. For the Matteawan Mannerchor, posed here on a hillside off Verplanck Avenue, German songs were a specialty.

THE SUNBONNET GIRLS, C. 1910. Irish immigrants came to this community in the 19th century, found jobs as servants and laborers, worked hard, and soon became some of the most successful businessmen of the town—men such as Frank Timoney, John Flannery, and James Forrestal. Irish women may have had fewer opportunities but they worked equally hard. Pictured are the daughters of first-generation Irish-Americans—girls with names like Lynch, Keating, Collins, and Heaney. These girls would play their own parts in shaping Beacon's future.

MAIN STREET PARADE, 1919. Among the Beaconites who turned out to welcome home veterans of Word War I, were members of the "Czechoslovakian Society of Beacon." By 1930, 49.9 percent of Beacon's population was either foreign-born or of foreign parentage. A microcosm of the American melting pot, Beacon absorbed many different nationalities into its citizenry over the decades—through fluctuating waves of immigration that brought new Americans from Ireland, Italy, Czechoslovakia, and many other lands to our shore.

PARADE PARTICIPANTS, 1919. The blending of old-world custom with new-world tradition is obvious in the costumes donned by marchers in the World War I "Welcome Home" parade which said "thank you" to the Beaconites who had fought on foreign soil to protect small-town American life. Elizabeth Sylvanie, Rita Frederick, Catherine Sherrilla, Concetta Palisi, Miss Shevetone, Louie Moscato, and Angelina Rossi posed aside the Sylvanie's home located near the corner of Main and South Chestnut Streets.

St. Luke's Cadet Corps at St. Luke's Church, c. 1900. One of the more notable of the many St. Luke's Church parish organizations was the St. Luke's Cadet Corps, a crack drill team active in the early 1900s. Under the direction of drillmaster Capt. Fred Ives, the nattily attired Cadet Corps put on marching exhibitions and exacting drill maneuvers at public events. Later, the cadets expanded into a drum and bugle corps, many of whose members would breakaway to form the Chanler Drum Corps.

Christmas at the Scofield House, 1902. The Scofield and Tompkins family relatives gather round the tree in the parlor of the Scofield home on Tioronda Avenue to celebrate Christmas. Marion Scofield is the little girl on her father's lap. The tall Santa is her uncle, George Tompkins. The tree is decorated with candles, popcorn, tinsel, and period ornaments. And Christmas dinner in a typical Victorian household like the Scofield's most likely would be roasted chicken, duck, or goose.

DUTCHESS FIFE, DRUM AND BUGLE CORPS, C. 1910. Beacon has mounted a half-dozen different drum corps over the parade of time. The first in line, and one of the longest-lived, was the Dutchess Fife, Drum and Bugle Corps. Dutchess Fife was organized in 1884, to travel to Washington, D.C., to play for the Grand Army of the Republic. Seven decades later the corps was still together and was known as the oldest musical organization of its kind in the state still in existence.

CHANLER FIFE, DRUM AND BUGLE CORPS, 1910. One of the oldest active drum corps in the state is the Chanler Drum and Bugle Corps of Beacon. Organized in Matteawan in 1903, Chanler's took the name of its first benefactor—Lewis Stuyvesant Chanler, a lieutenant governor of New York who donated money to the group. The corps, dressed in its distinctive green and white uniforms, would earn many parade trophies and honors, highlighted by their appearance at half-time in the 1959 Orange Bowl.

EXCURSION TO DENNING'S POINT, C. 1900. Horseplay and hijinks abound as this group of young people cavorts for the camera on an outing to Denning's Point. By the turn of the century the point had become widely known as a picnic spot and swimming hole. "Denning's Point has become the Coney Island of Dutchess County," the *Fishkill Standard* newspaper reported. "Not a day passes when this fine little beach is not covered with picnic parties from Matteawan, Fishkill Landing, and Newburgh."

THE BUDD FAMILY'S NEW AUTOMOBILE, C. 1915. Members of the Budd family of Maple Street in Beacon sidle up to their new car. The purchase of a new automobile in the early years of motoring often made the local paper as important social news. And of course you did not have to know how to drive a car in order to buy one—after the sale, the dealer would take the new owner out for a few hours of practice and, ready or not, he or she was licensed to drive!

SWIMMING AT DENNING'S POINT, 1931. For decades, right up to the 1940s, the Denning's Point beach was a summertime attraction. The *Beacon Light* newspaper in July of 1931 noted the Point's appeal: "Every day this resort becomes more popular. There is dancing every Sunday starting at 2 o'clock. The fine dance floor and excellent music is an attraction. A motorboat now runs from Newburgh, and hundreds of people came across the river to picnic, enjoy the bathing and the other amusements now at the Point."

OUTING AT CHASE'S GROVE, GLENHAM, 1920. One of the most popular spots for Beacon clubs and organizations to hold a clambake, bazaar, or other outdoor outing was Chase's Grove, located along the Fishkill Creek in Glenham. Summer was the season for such outings, and August was the favorite month for clambakes, with corn on the cob on the side and plenty of beer to wash it down. After working six days a week, these men had earned a summer Sunday of enjoyment.

NRA PARADE, OCTOBER 13, 1933. Who's Afraid of the Big Bad Wolf (Depression), anyway? Not Beacon: rallying around the banner of the Blue Eagle, the symbol of FDR's National Recovery Administration, were 3,500 marchers, dozens of floats, and ten thousand spectators—all to show support for the New Deal program designed to spur on the nation's economy. But mostly the parade was a morale booster, a chance for Beaconites to dress up and proclaim, "Who's afraid?"

FDR AT BANK SQUARE, 1936. Not since Teddy Roosevelt came to town as the Bull Moose candidate had a president campaigned in Beacon. That changed when the other Roosevelt—Franklin Delano—made his coming to Beacon on election eve a campaign tradition. In fact, FDR had made his very first political speech here. Such was his popularity that thousands packed Bank Square on November 2, 1936, to see Roosevelt address "his old neighbors of Beacon."

NICKELS FOR A NEW REFRIGERATOR, 1938. "Buy a new refrigerator for only two nickels a day!" The hard times of the Depression forced businesses to adopt new strategies, like this ad-line, to attract customers. Central Hudson took this picture of Beacon's Betty Morse with her twins, Billy and Betty, and daughter Priscilla, at home with their new Westinghouse refrigerator to advertise their "Meter-Ice Plan": you placed two nickels a day into a box attached to the refrigerator, and in four years it was yours!

ST. JOHN'S BOY SCOUT TROOP 21, 1939. Federal Court Judge Edward Conger cuts the cake as the guest of honor at the first anniversary party of Troop 21 at St. John's church hall—with future mayor Bob Cahill front and center. Beacon had the first Boy Scout troop in Dutchess County—old Troop 1, founded in 1911 by noted author and explorer Dillon Wallace of Beacon (who served as its first scoutmaster). Wallace later served on the National Scout Council, and was instrumental in bringing the scout movement to America.

Old Gown Exhibit by Members of Melzingah Chapter, DAR, c. 1938. Founded in Fishkill Landing in 1896, the Melzingah Chapter of the DAR drew its name from a Native American word associated with the area and believed to mean "spirit of the waters." Members gathered here at Roseneath (estate of Founding Regent Katherine Wolcott Verplanck) include then-Regent Geraldine Cunningham (front row, fourth from the left). The Chapter's membership also once included the Countess Lavenia Warren Magri, perhaps better known as Mrs. Tom Thumb. A pair of her tiny shoes is still on display at the Chapter's Homestead.

Mayor Lewis Bolton and Actress Gloria Swanson, June 1947. After World War II, the "Original Van Wyck Players," brought fine drama and a host of noted Hollywood actors to Beacon's Roosevelt Theatre. The Roosevelt had opened in 1934 with the aspiration of becoming the finest theater in the Hudson Valley. Gloria Swanson was one of many acting legends (including John Carradine, Conrad Nagle, Miriam Hopkins, and Zasu Pitts) who stepped into the footlights of its stage.

MELIO BETTINA—LIGHT HEAVYWEIGHT CHAMPION, 1939. The proudest moment in Beacon's sports history was when favorite son Melio Bettina knocked out Tiger Jack Fox in the ninth round at Madison Square Garden to become the Light Heavyweight Champion of the World. Some two thousand Beacon fans rode the "Bettina Special" train to New York that February 3rd to lend raucous support for Melio and later to celebrate his victory. In 1995 Melio was inducted into the World Boxing Hall of Fame.

MELIO BETTINA
Former World's Light Heavyweight Champion

BEACON BEARS, 1947. Beginning in the mid-1930s for two decades (with a short break during World War II), Beacon boasted its own semi-professional football team, the Beacon Bears. Thousands of fans turned out for Memorial Field games against squads from other parts of the Hudson Valley, Connecticut, and New Jersey. But the advent of television soon meant those same fans could instead spend their Sundays at home, watching the real pros. With few fans and even fewer players, the team folded in 1957.

PHOTOGRAPHERS AT GROVEVILLE PARK, C. 1888. Among the pioneer photographers gathered at the Union Sunday school picnic were Charles Palmer, Egbert Conklin, Fred Budd, and John Post—men who captured via tintype, daguerreotype, and photograph some of the very images within this volume. Later generations of their breed included such men as Harry Van Tine, Robert W. Murphy, and Ralph Morse. It would be impossible to appreciate the chapters of our past were it not for their collective contribution to documenting that history. To these men and others like them, we express our gratitude; and to city historian Joan K. VanVoorhis, our particular thanks for sharing her wealth of knowledge and enthusiasm for Beacon's story.

We also note our appreciation to the following people and institutions that helped in a thousand small ways to make this book a reality:

Chuck Benjamin
Janet Barresi
Gladys Bettina
Vivian Bolton
Central Hudson Gas & Electric Corporation
Derry Dubetsky
Nick Francese
Historical Society of Newburgh Bay & the Highlands
Lewis Tompkins Hose Company
Ed Maxim
Austin McEntee
Melzingah Chapter, NSDAR

Jim Moseman
Diane Murphy
Ludwig Ruf
Jill Sammon
Fred Simmonds
Jackson Stearns
Nancy Siebert
Douglas Story
Gordon Ticehurst
Steven VanBuren
Larry Way
Vernon Way

and all those members and friends who have contributed to the archives of the Beacon Historical Society by donating family treasures and historical photographs.

Robert J. Murphy
President
Beacon Historical Society

Denise Doring VanBuren
Regent
Melzingah Chapter, NSDAR